P9-DXM-917

the SELF-ACCEPTANCE PROJECT

the SELF-ACCEPTANCE PROJECT

How to Be
Kind & Compassionate
Toward Yourself
in Any Situation

an anthology edited by Tami Simon

SOUNDS TRUE
BOULDER, COLORADO

Sounds True
Boulder, CO 80306

This work is solely for personal growth and education. It should not be treated as a substitute for professional assistance such as psychotherapy, counseling, or medical advice. In the event of physical or mental distress, please consult with appropriate health-care professionals.

Published 2016

Cover design by Rachael Murray
Book design by Beth Skelley
Cover image © Ullithemrg, shutterstock.com

"Breaking Surface" by Mark Nepo is reprinted with permission from the author.

Printed in Canada

Library of Congress Cataloging-in-Publication Data
Names: Simon, Tami, editor.
Title: The self-acceptance project : how to be kind and compassionate toward
    yourself in any situation / edited by Tami Simon.
Description: Boulder, CO : Sounds True, 2016. | Includes bibliographical references.
Identifiers: LCCN 2015038172 | ISBN 9781622034673 (alk. paper)
Subjects: LCSH: Self-acceptance.
Classification: LCC BF575.S37 S45 2015 | DDC 158.1—dc23
LC record available at http://lccn.loc.gov/2015038172

EBook ISBN 978-1-62203-630-1   33614056495350

10 9 8 7 6 5 4 3 2 1

CONTENTS

EMBODYING SELF-ACCEPTANCE

AWAKENING SELF-ACCEPTANCE

INTRODUCTION

Tami Simon

Founder and Publisher, Sounds True

I t's hard to be kind to yourself. At least that is my experience, especially when difficult things happen.

Early on in my life, I discovered that there was a part of me that turned against myself when something unfortunate happened that I perceived to be my fault—perhaps a misstep or something that felt like a failure. The first time this became painfully obvious was when I was twenty-two years old and had just launched Sounds True.

It's a long story, but the gist of it is that I decided it would be a terrific idea to produce and host a Soviet-American citizen's summit for public radio as an extension of Sounds True's conference-recording service. The broadcast was a chance for public radio listeners to hear Russian citizens in dialogue with Americans to illustrate how everyday people can become ambassadors of peace and goodwill. The broadcast itself was well done, and the content flowed seamlessly. There was only one problem, and it was a *big* problem: the translation feed did not come through to the broadcast audience. This meant when participants spoke in Russian (which was about twenty-five minutes of the hour-long production), listeners did not hear any English translation; they heard only the original Russian language. In other words, the live broadcast to tens of thousands of people was largely incomprehensible.

As producer and host, I was devastated and humiliated. People tried to console me: "It is good for people to hear a language that is unfamiliar. You provided a public service." But inside, I felt like I wanted to die. Yes, end my life right there on the spot. I couldn't take a full breath. I wanted to crawl under a rock and never come out. Instead, I crawled into my hotel bed (if there had been room *under* the bed,

I would have crawled there), and I squeezed myself into a tight ball for about twenty-four hours. There was no comfort there, only a terrible voice inside that said things like "You should kill yourself now." I made a decision at that time to never produce and host a live broadcast event again. The potential pain of that type of failure was too much for me to bear. I only wanted to work on projects that I could polish and make perfect ("perfect" being the operative word). It was just too painful to do something that carried with it the risk of public humiliation.

Years later, this event from my young life as a producer and host receded into the background, and with it, the pain. However, I was left with two important discoveries: first, that I was determined to design my life to avoid such "failures" at all cost, and second, that I had a terribly mean voice inside that responded to difficult situations by punishing me and declaring that it would be useless for me to continue living. To say this voice was self-aggressive was an understatement. This voice spoke to me in a way that I could never imagine speaking to another person, yet it lived *in* me and had the potential to turn on me if things didn't go well.

As the years passed, I started to recognize this inner voice as a type of sub-personality (some people call it "the inner critic" or "the judge") that seemed to have its own life. It would become active and vocal when something seemingly went wrong. This critical voice would even tear me to shreds over small and insignificant things—like cooking a meal for friends and putting too much salt in the food—and then I would have a sleepless night listening to it berate me. "Really?" I thought, "Over something like this? You've got to be kidding me."

With time, I started to take this voice less and less seriously—it was so out of step with the actual magnitude of situations. Through a lot of inner work, both in one-on-one therapy and on the meditation cushion, the voice gradually began to lose its power. I could still hear it, but it was no longer in charge of my state of being. Other capacities came on board, including the capacity to be kind to myself and offer myself comfort. I even became curious about this voice's origin and purpose: What function might it be serving in the total ecology of my psyche? What were the emotions, and the accompanying physical sensations, that lay waiting for me underneath the voice? Could I turn toward those emotions and sensations with openness and curiosity?

I also became intensely curious about other people's experiences with self-criticism and self-judgment. How was it that some people made mistakes and viewed the entire experience as a learning opportunity? How could I become more like those types of people?

In parallel to my own growing curiosity about self-acceptance, I began working with people as a meditation instructor. In private meetings, people shared their innermost struggles with me. What often impacted me the most was how hard people were on themselves, how negative self-talk was more the norm than the exception. Very often, people had an overlay of self-judgment when they were in the midst of a difficult experience. Again and again, I heard people say, "I am suffering in this way, and I feel like I am a terrible person because I am suffering in this way."

From those conversations, I saw that people judged themselves for so many different kinds of things—for being too fat or too thin, for being too verbal or not verbal enough, for being closed-hearted or too open and porous. People judged themselves about their past—if only this or that had or hadn't happened. People judged their sexual orientation or lack of a sexual orientation. People judged themselves for being too old, too this or too that, for not being "enough" of something or other. And people endlessly compared themselves to other people and mythic ideals. People had internalized voices of judgment about everything that they were and that they weren't.

Working with meditation students, I also saw how self-judgment kept people from taking risks. It often felt like a lid that people used to keep themselves safe, small, contained, and under-potentiated. And this was painful to see—how sensitive, good-hearted human beings often focus on what they supposedly lack instead of their beauty, strength, possibility, and power to create.

I started to see "unconditional self-acceptance"—being kind to ourselves no matter what is happening in our lives—as an immensely powerful life skill that most of us have not been taught. I started to see that being kind to ourselves is actually a human capacity that changes everything. It changes how we treat ourselves day to day, how we take risks, how we love, how we create, and how we make space for what seems "unacceptable" in others.

Over time, I came to see being kind to ourselves as quite an advanced practice. I call it an "advanced practice" because I found myself in conversation with people who had been on a path of personal growth for decades—people who had been meditating or in therapy for years—who still found it quite challenging to treat themselves with kindness when confronted with certain situations. And I wanted to know more about what makes self-acceptance so difficult for so many of us and, more importantly, how we can develop this capacity widely and broadly, individually and collectively, as a way to release waves and waves of kindness.

The Self-Acceptance Project was born out of this inquiry. Originally created for online broadcast—hey, I started doing live broadcasts again!—*The Self-Acceptance Project* originated as a series of interviews with psychologists, dharma teachers, neurobiologists, writers, and educators on the essential keys to being kind and compassionate toward ourselves, especially on the spot in difficult situations. The book you are reading now is derived from this original series of interviews.

The very good news that *The Self-Acceptance Project* delivers is that there is a lot to learn about self-acceptance that can be intensely and immediately helpful: accepting the part of ourselves that is not self-accepting, understanding how our brains are wired to look for what is wrong (known as the *negativity bias*), learning to immediately respond and talk to ourselves in self-loving ways when in the midst of a challenge, and more. *The Self-Acceptance Project* also helps us realize that feeling inadequate at times is not something unique to us; it is a feeling that many, many of us share.

When the broadcast of the original interview series was complete, I received hundreds of letters from people who listened and found the interviews extraordinarily helpful. What I learned from these letters is that people were immensely grateful that some of their favorite authors and teachers were not just offering their advice and techniques for cultivating self-acceptance, they were sharing their own struggles and journeys that had unfolded in their lives to help them develop self-acceptance first hand. The series was tremendously *normalizing* for listeners, and I hope this book will have the same impact on you. When we learn how our difficulties are shared, even by the people we admire (and sometimes "pedestalize"), we embrace our humanness. We see that our struggles are shared human struggles, part of the human condition. We have the opportunity to relax with being human.

I am convinced that the more accepting we are of ourselves, the more accepting we will be of other people. If there are parts of ourselves that we disown, push away, and deem unacceptable, then we will be unwilling and unable to make room to receive and embrace those aspects of other people. Ultimately, the work of *The Self-Acceptance Project* is not just about you and me learning to work with ourselves in a loving and kind way. It is about learning how to relate to, and be with, anyone—and I mean *anyone*—in a loving and kind way. When we are able to be with our own difficulties and intense experiences that are seemingly unwanted, then we can be with other people's difficulties and their seemingly unwanted experiences. *The Self-Acceptance Project* is about having the bravery to open our hearts to ourselves—and to everyone and everything.

When we develop a strong sense of self-acceptance, we become capable of such bravery. We may still hear critical inner voices, but they no longer hold power over us. We move forward anyway. We develop the courage to take risks and to stand in our truth because we become more confident that we can handle it if our risk-taking leads to disappointment or disapproval. We so thoroughly befriend ourselves that we can risk receiving criticism, looking like a failure, or suffering loss. Brave people create, brave people speak up, brave people call bullshit "bullshit," brave people bring their hearts forward and put their hearts on the line, brave people love outrageously. May *The Self-Acceptance Project* help you become such a brave person!

practicing
SELF-ACCEPTANCE

WAKING UP FROM THE
TRANCE OF UNWORTHINESS

Tara Brach

*Building a true sense of self-trust comes from making contact
with the deeper parts of our being, such as the truth of our
loving, even when we sometimes act in ways we don't like.*

Many years ago, I began to focus on the urgent need for self-acceptance. In fact, I called it *radical* self-acceptance, because the notion of holding oneself with love and compassion was still so foreign. It had become clear to me that a key part of my emotional suffering was a sense of feeling "not enough," which, at times, escalated into full-blown self-aversion. As I witnessed similar patterns in my students and clients, I began to realize that the absence of self-acceptance is one of the most pervasive expressions of suffering in our society.

We can spend huge swaths of our life living in what I call the "trance of unworthiness," trapped in a chronic sense of falling short. Though we're rarely conscious of it, we continually evaluate ourselves. So often, we perceive a gap between the person we believe we should be and our actual moment-to-moment experience. This gap makes us feel as if we're always, in some way, *not* okay. As if we're inherently deficient. A palliative caregiver who has worked with thousands of dying people once wrote that the deepest regret expressed by her patients is that they hadn't been true to themselves. They'd lived according to the expectations of others, according to the *should*, but not aligned with their own hearts.

That speaks volumes. We can move through our days so out of touch with ourselves that, at the end, we feel sorrow for not having expressed our own aliveness, creativity, and love.

So much of the time we're simply unaware of just how pervasive that sense of *something's-wrong-with-me* is. Like an undetected toxin, it can infect every aspect of our lives. For example, in relationships, we may wear ourselves out trying to make others perceive us in a certain way—smart, beautiful, spiritual, powerful, whatever our personal ideal happens to be. We want them to approve of us, love us. Yet, it's very hard to be intimate when, at some deep level, we feel flawed or deficient. It's hard to be spontaneous or creative or take risks—or even relax in the moment—if we think that we're falling short.

From an evolutionary perspective, a sense of vulnerability is natural. Fearing that something's wrong or about to go wrong is part of the survival instinct that keeps us safe—a good thing when we're being chased by a grizzly bear! Although this sense of vulnerability—of being threatened—is innately human, all too often we turn it in on ourselves. Our self-consciousness makes it personal. We move quickly from "Something is wrong or bad," to "*I'm* the one who's wrong or bad." This is the nature of our unconscious, self-reflexive awareness; we automatically tend to identify with what's deficient. In psychological parlance, this scanning for and fixating on what is wrong is described as "negativity bias."

For most of us, our feelings of deficiency were underscored by messages we received in childhood. We were told how to behave and what kinds of looks, personality, and achievements would lead to success, approval, and love. Rarely do any of us grow up feeling truly loveable and worthy just as we are.

Our contemporary culture further exacerbates our feelings of inadequacy. There are few natural ways of belonging that help to reassure us about our basic goodness, few opportunities to connect to something larger than ourselves. Ours is a fear-based society that over-consumes, is highly competitive, and sets standards valuing particular types of intelligence, body types, and achievements. Because the standards are set by the dominant culture, the message of inferiority is especially painful for people of color and others who are continually faced with being considered "less than" due to appearance, religion, sexual or gender orientation, or socio-economic status.

When we believe that something is inherently wrong with us, we expect to be rejected, abandoned, and separated from others. In reaction, the more primitive parts of our brain devise strategies to defend or promote ourselves. We take on chronic self-improvement projects. We exaggerate, lie, or pretend to be something we're not in order to cover our feelings of unworthiness. We judge and behave aggressively toward others. We turn on ourselves.

Although it's natural to try to protect ourselves with such strategies, the more evolved parts of our brain offer another option: the capacity to tend and befriend. Despite our conditioning, we each have the potential for mindful presence and unconditional love. *Once we see the trance of unworthiness—how we're suffering because we're at war with our self—we can commit to embracing the totality of our inner experience.* This commitment, along with a purposeful training in mindfulness and compassion, can transform our relationship with all of life.

It's helpful to understand that when we're possessed by fearful reactivity, we can be hijacked by our primitive brain and disconnected from the neuro-circuitry that correlates with mindfulness and compassion. We become cut off from the very parts of ourselves that allow us to trust ourselves, to be more happy and free. The critical inquiry is what enables us to reconnect—to regain access to our most evolved, cherished human qualities.

The gateway is the direct experience of the suffering of fear and shame that have been driving us. Not long ago, one of my students revealed that she felt as if she could never be genuinely intimate with another person because she was afraid that if anyone really knew her, they'd reject her outright. This woman had spent her whole life believing, "I'll be rejected if somebody sees who I am." It wasn't until she acknowledged her pain and viewed it as a wake-up call that she could begin to stop the war against herself.

Once we recognize our suffering, the first step toward healing is learning to pause. We might think, "I'm unworthy of my partner's love because I'm a selfish person." Or, "I'm unworthy because I'm not a fun or spontaneous person." Or perhaps, "I don't deserve love because I always let people down." We might experience feelings of shame or fear or hopelessness. Whatever our experience, learning to pause when we're caught in our suffering is the critical first step. As Holocaust survivor and psychiatrist Viktor Frankl famously said: "Between stimulus and response, there is a space. In that space is our power to choose our response. In our response lies our growth and freedom." When we pause, we can respond to the prison of our beliefs and feelings in a healing way.

The second step toward healing is to deepen attention. It's important to ask, "Beneath all of my negative thoughts, what's going on in my body, in my heart, right now?" When we begin to bring awareness to the underlying pain, I sometimes call that the sense of *"ouch."* You might even ask how long it's been going on and realize: "Wow. I've been feeling *not enough* for as long as I can remember." If that happens, try placing your hand on your heart as a sign of your intention to be kind toward yourself and your suffering. You might even tell yourself, "I want to be able to be gentle with this place inside me that feels so bad."

For most of us, staying with the "ouch" can be painful and grueling; it can wear down our spirit and energy. The reason I suggest putting a hand on our heart is that a gesture toward ourselves that expresses comfort or healing has real power. If being with yourself in that way is uncomfortable, imagine someone who is truly wise and compassionate helping you; this can serve as a bridge to bringing the healing presence to yourself.

When we do this, a shift begins to occur. We move from being identified with the unworthy self to a compassionate presence that witnesses and is *with* the unworthy self. That shift is a movement toward freedom. It's in that very moment when we become present and offer kindness—or the intention of kindness—to ourselves that real transformation begins to take place.

I've experienced many triggers for my own trance of unworthiness. One of the most powerful in recent years was a long stretch of illness. Not only did I feel sick, but I would often become irritable and self-centered, then stop liking myself for being a bad sick person. It felt as if I were not being very spiritually mature in dealing with my illness. The Buddha called this the second arrow. The first arrow is, "Oh, I feel sick." In other words, just what is. The second arrow is the sense of unworthiness we inflict upon ourselves—in my case, being a bad *sick* person.

When I experienced a sense of personal failure, of not being a good person, I'd pause, put my hand on my heart, and imagine an understanding presence around me, pouring care through my hands. Sometimes I'd mentally whisper the words "It's okay, sweetheart" or "I'm sorry, and I love you." Although at first I was invoking a larger presence to offer care to the bad sick person, as I relaxed, it became clear that the loving presence I'd invoked was intrinsic to my own heart.

This process of reconnecting to our sense of goodness and worthiness that I've described is based on two key elements—mindful recognition of what's going on inside us, and a compassionate response. Many people have found that the practice of R-A-I-N offers an easy way to do this:

- R is to *recognize* what's going on. Pause and acknowledge all the thoughts and feelings of unworthiness.

- A is to *allow*, which means we allow the thoughts and feelings to be there. We deepen the pause. We don't try to distract ourselves or get away from what's happening. We let it just be, so that we can deepen into the "I" of RAIN.

- I is to *investigate* with kindness. We bring a gentle, yet interested attention to our experience. This is where we start loosening the grip of the trance. Here's where you can put your hand on your heart and offer yourself a message of compassion, or open to receive the loving presence from the larger energy field to which we belong.

- N means *not-identified*. This may sound like a dry term, but it signifies true liberation. When we don't identify with that unworthy self, we're free to inhabit our wholeness, free to inhabit the loving awareness that was clouded over, but always there.

RAIN is a process of disentangling from the trance. What it really comes down to is mindful awareness with kindness. The more I practice RAIN in my own life, the less lag time there is between getting stuck and relaxing open into a larger, freer sense of being. RAIN has helped me catch the ideas and feelings that have to do with an unworthy self, and then to realize that I don't have to believe them! The feelings are there, the thoughts are there, but the sense of who I am is beyond any limiting story of self. I've learned to trust the *beingness* that is here, a loving presence that isn't stained or diminished by thoughts or feelings of unworthiness.

I've seen how, for myself and many others, even when we've been filled with self-hate or blame, we can find our way back to kindness. A metaphor I find helpful is to imagine you're in the woods and you see a dog by a tree. You go over to pet the sweet dog and it springs at you suddenly—growling, with fangs bared. In an instant, you switch from wanting to pet the puppy to being really angry and afraid. Then you notice that the dog has caught its leg in a trap under a pile of leaves, so you switch again, from anger and fear to care and compassion. If we can pause and recognize that in some way our leg is in a trap, if we can see that the behavior we've been harshly judging in ourselves is coming from our pain, then we soften. We regain access to a natural tenderness toward our own suffering, and with that, open back into a more full and compassionate presence toward all beings.

Along with recognizing our vulnerability, self-acceptance arises as we deepen trust in our essential goodness. A woman once came up to me after a class and said, "I'm at war with myself because of the way I'm treating my five-year-old daughter. I'm bursting out in anger all the time and criticizing her, and I don't deserve to accept myself. How can I trust myself if I'm doing this?" She was afraid that accepting or forgiving herself would just perpetuate being a bad mother. We all act in ways that are harmful at times, and reacting with self-punishment and self-hate is not a pathway toward more wise behavior.

I asked her, "Do you love your daughter?"

Tears sprang up as she answered. "Of course! I wouldn't be so upset about this if I didn't love my daughter."

"Spend some time reflecting on loving her, what you love about her," I suggested. "Feel that loving awareness in you, and get to know *that* as the place you can trust."

That really resonated with her because intuitively she understood that while she couldn't trust her ego, she could trust her heart. If we think we should be able to trust our ego-self, it's not going to work. The ego-self is unreliable, out of control, causes trouble, strives, and is afraid. Building a true sense of self-trust comes from making contact with the deeper parts of our being, such as the truth of our loving, even when we sometimes act in ways we don't like.

We are each on a path of awakening to loving the life that is here. Though we might call it self-acceptance, what we're accepting is this feeling—this hurt, this sadness, this fear, this anxiety, and this sense of doing something wrong. As we grow to accept and embrace this living reality—its pleasantness, its unpleasantness—the illusion of a separate self dissolves. We discover the radiance and love that is our essence. The more we trust this essence, the more we recognize that same goodness and spirit in all beings. Our embrace of our inner life widens to an authentic and unconditional love for this living world.

2

HEALING AT THE LEVEL OF THE SUBCONSCIOUS MIND

Friedemann Schaub

*The good news is that pain, whether physical
or emotional, can function as a powerful catalyst
for healing, change, and growth.*

The discussion about the absence of self-compassion and self-acceptance may be even more imperative now than it had been for previous generations. The demands of modern society have trained us to constantly comply, compete, and compare ourselves with others and consequently derive our worthiness mainly through external perspectives, judgments, and validations. Life is no longer considered a journey—it has become a competition, a race, with no apparent reward or finish line to reach.

This externally focused way of living has been accelerated by the omnipresent media, increased societal pressures, and new ways of communicating that prevent us from taking the time to relax and develop a relationship with ourselves. Consequently, we feel increasingly pulled out of our center and lose touch with our authentic selves. We no longer search for our truth, our unique potential, and our purpose for being here. Most of our energy goes to competing, winning, or at least "fitting in," instead of exploring the unique gifts and talents we can express and share with the world.

The dramatic increase in the number of people suffering from fear, anxiety, and depression in the last decades is a direct reflection of how many of us struggle with the painful lack of inner peace and self-acceptance. The good news is that pain, whether physical or emotional, can function as a powerful catalyst for healing, change, and growth. The current level of pain, anxiety, and depression in our society offers a huge opportunity for growth on a larger scale, and it is encouraging to see that more and more people recognize that the path to harmony, peace, and fulfillment leads them within.

One of the first steps toward self-acceptance and self-compassion is to become aware of how our self-talk can be based in judgment, worry, and self-doubt. Without hesitation or remorse, we scare ourselves, put ourselves down, and even call ourselves names in ways we would never dare to treat anyone else, especially not someone we care about. But what can we do to make this insecure, critical, or negative inner voice stop? Should we ignore it, get angry, and fight it—or should we accept that its self-berating or self-doubting messages are true?

In my practice, I am helping people to understand how our subconscious influences our emotions and behaviors—and how we can access this deeper part of our mind to overcome and heal fear, anxiety, and depression. One of the keys to healing these emotional challenges is to identify and address the subconscious self-protective patterns, which keep us in survival mode and prevent us from thriving and living more fulfilling lives. Most of our negative self-talk stems from our subconscious mind. It is important to understand that the purpose of those self-bashing, anxiety-triggering thoughts is not to hurt us or to make us feel bad about ourselves. The purpose of this inner voice is ultimately to protect us.

When we listen to our negative monologue, we may sometimes hear echoes of our childhood. Some of my clients tell me their inner critic sounds exactly like their father or uncle or teacher. Others feel that the inner voice that always expects the other shoe to drop reminds them of their anxious mothers or grandmothers. Our subconscious mind replays those tapes of the past to prevent us from having to endure failure, hurt, rejection, or abandonment. Let's say, for example, whenever you have a new idea or want to make a change, a voice pipes up in your head: "Oh no, you shouldn't do this because people will not like it; you better not even try" or "Who do you think you are? You don't have what it takes to succeed."

Although this inner naysayer may appear quite negative and critical, all it attempts to do is to protect you through making you want to be invisible and avoid anything that potentially could make you a target for the criticism and rejection of others. Or, maybe there's a voice that always asks, "Are you sure this person likes you? Maybe next time you should try X, Y, and Z to make him happier." This pleaser pattern tries to keep you safe by making sure that everyone approves of you. When you recognize that the anxious or self-demeaning voice just tries to prevent you from having to go through pain and suffering, you gain more acceptance, compassion, and maybe even appreciation for this subconscious part that tries so hard to keep you safe and alive.

You could say that the inner protector is somewhat stuck in the past. From its perspective, nothing has changed: the world is still scary and unpredictable, and you're still small, vulnerable, and cannot take care of yourself. There is often a disconnection between you—the competent adult—and that part of you that started to develop when you were still a child. This disconnection creates a distorted perspective on reality. Your adult side might say, "I can write a book" or "I can get a promotion" or "I can go on a date with that gorgeous person." But your inner protector doesn't believe you can do those things and holds on to the notion that you are much better off when you remain small and safe in your comfort zone and don't try to put yourself out there.

To resolve this disconnect or fragmentation of your mind, you need to update your programming and start convincing your subconscious mind that you're no longer the small, powerless person of the past, whom it still tries to protect. How do you start conveying to your subconscious that you are a strong, well-resourced adult, who can handle any situation you are facing? First, *you* have to be convinced that this empowered perception of yourself is true. If you are not convinced yet, ask yourself, "What do I know about myself that I can believe in, that I can appreciate? How many times have I proved to myself that I can overcome obstacles and accomplish what I intended to? And what were the innate qualities and strengths that allowed me to reach my goals?" Take a little inventory of your successes, gifts, and talents to boost your awareness that you are truly no longer a helpless child.

Next, you need to address and redirect the voice of your negative self-talk. If you just try to ignore or shut down this anxious, insecure part, you may end up creating an even greater internal disconnect. Instead, help it to break through the illusion of not being good enough or not being safe by presenting it with the evidence of your more positive and self-empowered adult reality. For example, negative self-talk often generalizes, "I always fail" or "I will never be able to have what I want" or "I only had misfortune in my life," and ignores all the evidence that could show that the opposite is true. When you are addressing such anxiety-triggering thoughts, imagine that you are talking to someone who is scared and concerned about you. Your job is to point out the positive aspects of yourself and your life, to convince that person that his or her negative perspective is a distortion of your reality.

Now keep in mind that you cannot address your inner protector with just logic and rational arguments. Starting a debating club with yourself doesn't work. Instead, approach that subconscious part from your heart, with compassion and kindness. I find it very powerful to visualize that inner protector as a younger version of yourself, who feels just as scared, worried, and powerless as you did when you were a child. Comfort and reassure this part by redirecting its negative thoughts toward an awareness of positivity and possibility.

You could, for example, carry a photograph with you, which shows you at the age of seven or eight or during a time when you felt the most insecure and anxious. Imagine that the source of most of your negative self-talk is like the kid in the photograph. How would you comfort and reassure that younger self after you heard its anxious voice? What guidance would you give that child, so that he or she can perceive reality in a more hopeful and positive way?

Through this form of compassionate inner communication, you are creating a connection between the adult self and the child self that still feels trapped in the past. This simple exercise is so effective that for most of my clients, their negative self-talk drops by an average of 80 percent within just two to three weeks. At some point, most people no longer hear any negative self-talk, because they feel that the voice that tried to get their attention has finally received the reassurance and caring support it needed.

Here is a specific example. One of my clients, Bob, was what you could call an overachiever. Every time he reached a goal, he immediately started aiming for a higher one. This was not because of pure ambition or a sense of joy and purpose, but because his lack of confidence and self-worth demanded he prove himself repeatedly.

However, with every success, his insecurities and worries of being found out as a fraud, and then losing everything he had, only increased. When he reached his ultimate goal to be the head of his corporate division, all of a sudden he started to suffer from severe panic attacks and insomnia. That's when Bob came to me for help. When we analyzed his self-talk, he realized that the internal voice that always tried to put him down and make him doubt himself had been with him since his early childhood. For most of his life, he had either ignored this voice or just worked harder to prove to himself that his insecurities were false.

As we went back into his childhood and examined the subconscious root cause of this critical voice, Bob remembered that he had seen his father, a simple man who had struggled all his life to make ends meet, as an underachiever. Being a sensitive young boy, he had felt and subconsciously absorbed his father's pain, anxiety, and self-limiting beliefs. As a result, his subconscious developed two parts. One, who identified Bob with his father's limiting beliefs of "I am not good enough" and "Life is hard and unfair." The other part was adamant about not ending up "stuck and broke" like him. The latter became the driving force for his relentless efforts to become the most successful member of his family. Yet, as hard as he tried, becoming an overachiever couldn't silence his insecurities. The more he accomplished, the louder the voice of doubt and worry became. He struggled with this inner conflict until his mid-forties, when he realized that living with such fragmentation was no longer sustainable.

Bob's example shows that your negative self-talk can stem from more than one source. Frequently, one subconscious part develops early in life, and the other later, often during adolescence. These parts can differ hugely in the way they try to protect you. While the initial inner protector may focus on avoiding danger and rejection through hiding out, becoming invisible, or pleasing others, the subconscious part that evolved later may focus on gaining respect and approval through success and achievements. It is also during this second phase of inner protection that a more controlling or rebellious part can emerge, which aims at disconnecting from the family fold or societal constraints, so that you can create your life undisturbed in your own way. It is quite powerful to identify those voices and to visualize and communicate with those inner younger selves at their different ages. Keep in mind that it is your opportunity and your *responsibility* as the loving, compassionate, and trustworthy adult to guide your inner protectors into the wholeness of the person you are now.

Through a re-integration process we did in one of our sessions, Bob was able to convince the avoider and the achiever parts that they didn't have to hold on to these old survival patterns, because the mature adult self has the resources and capabilities to keep himself—and them—safe. As if pieces of a puzzle that had been missing for a long time had finally fallen into their proper places, Bob felt from that moment on more whole and "himself" than he had ever before.

Although this healing concept may sound simple, the mere intellectual understanding is not enough. When it comes to self-acceptance, there is nothing more important than to be able to open your heart to yourself. Once you realize that the source of your negative self-talk, your inner tug-of-war, and lack of self-acceptance just need some reassurance and compassion, you will notice an enormous shift, because you start outgrowing your past. This is exactly what happened with Bob—he was able to heal and move beyond the past that he'd tried to run away from for decades. He found greater acceptance and appreciation for himself as he moved from his head, via the bridge of the subconscious mind, into his heart.

Have you ever noticed that your heart is wide open—just not to yourself? Some of the women I have worked with had stayed for years in emotionally and physically abusive relationships. It was only once their husbands were yelling at their children or laying hands on them that these women found the strength to leave their marriages. While they were willing to silently endure the pain that was inflicted on them, their love, concern, and compassion for their children gave them the courage to break out and start anew. Whether you are a loving parent, a loyal friend, or a deeply caring pet owner, in those relationships you have probably tapped into and expressed your innate capacity for compassion and open-heartedness countless times.

What may be more difficult for you is to open your heart toward yourself and give yourself the warmth, love, and caring energy that you share freely with others. This is where the connection to a younger inner self can be so eye- and heart-opening. Isn't it true that we can all have love and compassion for a child, especially when we realize that the child has been going through a difficult time? For example, Carol, another client of mine, constantly told herself that she wasn't good enough and that she didn't deserve to have fun or buy herself something nice. When we revisited her childhood, she remembered how she had always tried to please her anxious and depressed mother. As a young girl, she had convinced herself that to prevent her mother from being in pain, she had to shut down any desires or ambitions for herself and focus entirely on the needs of her mom. Now, looking back, Carol gained a new level of admiration and love for that young girl. She appreciated how much courage, compassion, and strength it took to make such a selfless decision. As she accepted and embraced little Carol, she started to soften her gaze and her heart toward herself.

Just like Carol, when you revisit your early years, you may also recognize that the reason why you may not have felt safe or good enough to express and be yourself was that you hadn't received enough love and compassion from others. As you are stepping into the role of the kind and caring adult who is willing and able to give that inner younger self what he or she has been longing for, you are well on your way to creating a new inner foundation of wholeness, harmony, and confidence.

To build a harmonious relationship with that younger self requires consistency, compassion, and patience. As with any child, you can't just show up once in a blue moon and address that anxious voice with a stern or irritable demeanor and then expect the inner child to trust you and let go of its old protective patterns. However, if you communicate with that younger self from your heart, with warmth, kindness, and nurturing energy, your negative self-talk will significantly decrease within a couple of weeks.

Communication doesn't always have to be verbal. It can also be visual. Visualize holding that child and imagine what it would feel like to have its little body in your arms. You can hold a pillow or embrace yourself, as you are opening your heart toward that most vulnerable part of you. Keep in mind that your subconscious doesn't distinguish between reality and imagination, which is why we can enjoy books and movies—and freak ourselves out about something that hasn't happened yet. When you're imagining that you're holding your younger self and giving him or her comfort and safety, your subconscious starts to release protective patterns it has held on to for a long time. And as this part expands beyond the past, you are essentially rewriting your story from seeing yourself as anxious, insecure, and unsafe to becoming the source of wholeness, love, and security. It continues to amaze me how impactful, profound, and permanent the healing work with the subconscious mind can be.

You can start your own healing journey toward growth and self-acceptance right now. The following exercise helps you to immediately interrupt the downward spiral of negative self-talk and build a trust-based relationship with your inner protector. It is very powerful and one of the most effective steps to start working with your subconscious mind.

- First notice and write down your negative thoughts as they bubble up from the depths of your subconscious. You don't even have to think about them. They're there. By paying attention, you already connect to that inner self that needs attention.

- The second step is to engage in a reality check and ask yourself the three questions:

Is this thought true?

Does this thought make me feel good?

Does this thought help me reach my goals?

These questions interrupt the spiral of negative thinking before it gets out of control.

- Now redirect the negative thought with three positive, counterbalancing thoughts. For example, if your thought is "I'm a failure," you can say, "I have succeeded in many things. There is no failure, just opportunities to grow and learn. I am a good person with good intentions." If you hear, "Something bad will happen," you could counterbalance with, "At this moment all is well. I have been anxious many times before and nothing bad happened. I have the inner resources to deal with anything that comes my way."

- Add compassionate, kind, and reassuring energy to the counterbalancing thoughts. For your subconscious mind, words only have any meaning and effect if they are associated with emotions. Rather than arguing with yourself in your head, engage your heart in this process. Even though it may appear difficult for you to be open and kind toward yourself, when you remember that the source of your negative thoughts is your inner younger protector who is just playing old "tapes" and repeating outdated survival programs, it becomes easier. By adding kindness and compassion to your counterbalancing positive thoughts, you take on the role of the competent and trustworthy adult. Assuming this role will shift your overall feeling from "I'm powerless and unsafe" to "I'm in charge of my safety and well-being."

As with all tools, this exercise works best when you practice it more than just one time. Remember, the goal is to create a consistent relationship with the source of your negative self-talk. Ideally, you want to repeat this process during the first month at least five times per day. Very quickly, you will notice a significant decrease in negative thoughts. It is as if your inner younger self has finally received the answers, guidance, and comfort it has been longing for. In response, you will no longer feel like the victim of your own thoughts, but experience a much greater sense of peace and self-acceptance.

3

BEAUTIFUL, NECESSARY, EXQUISITE EMOTIONS

Karla McLaren

Emotions are central to almost everything we think,
feel, and do. When we can accept our emotions,
then self–acceptance naturally follows.

As I study emotions and think about our obstacles to self-acceptance, it's clear that what I call "inauthentic" or foreign shame is a big culprit. However, another surprising obstacle is actually *empathy*. Empathy is a wonderful thing, but it can be a problem if we only use empathy with or for other people—and not for ourselves. Shame is also a wonderful thing, but it too can be a problem—a big problem—if we don't understand its purpose.

Many people are surprised when I say that empathy can be an obstacle to self-acceptance—because we usually think of empathy as entirely positive. No one would say, "I don't want any empathy." However, the troublesome thing about empathy is that, if we do it right, it should be completely and utterly about the other person; it's not about us. If what we do *is* about us, it's not really empathy—and if we're deeply empathic, we can spend so much time meeting the needs of others that we may "de-self" and lose empathy for ourselves. I see this in people who are very giving and often nearing burnout. When I ask, "If someone treated you the way you treat yourself, would you call the police?" The answer is often, "Yes! I would call the police *and* the fire department."

It doesn't need to be hard to be empathic toward ourselves if we're extremely empathic toward others, but it often is. I think this is because our ability to empathize starts so early. If we never learned about the need for self-empathy, we can grow up focusing totally on others and lose ourselves in the process. On the opposite side of that equation, we may learn how to *seem* to give to others, but not really hit the mark empathically. Betty Repacholi and Alison Gopnik at Berkeley created a wonderful study that illuminates the difference. They worked with babies and toddlers who were presented with two bowls: one with raw broccoli and one with goldfish crackers. All of the children loved the goldfish crackers. Only one or two liked the broccoli.

An adult experimenter came in and made a "yummy" face toward the broccoli and a "yucky" face toward the goldfish. In most cases, the experimenter was telling the child that she liked the opposite food (broccoli) to what the child wanted. Then, the experimenter, without cueing, would put her hand out and ask, "Can I have some food?" Some of the children wouldn't hand over anything, but many handed over the goldfish.

In this study, the giving of the goldfish was not seen as empathic, but as self-centered—because the child didn't meet the needs of the researcher. It was *generous* to hand over the goldfish (because the child liked goldfish), but it wasn't empathic. If the child handed over the broccoli, which the child didn't like at all, and maybe didn't even want to touch, that was identified as empathic. The study found that at a very early age—about eighteen months old—some children can understand that the needs of others can be completely different and even opposite to their own needs. They can meet those needs empathically—in this instance, by handing over the raw broccoli.

I love this experiment, because it demonstrates the difference between generosity and empathy. With empathy, you must almost "de-self" and get into the position of the other, take the other's perspective, and see what it is *they* want. Think about it in terms of giving gifts: Let's say that your friend loves the NFL but you can't stand football.

You love your friend, so you find the perfect gift that leans in to your friend's love of football.

Or, let's say that you're in a relationship with someone who needs a *lot* of attention, though you yourself are a reticent and quiet person. If you're very empathic, you may ignore or erase your own needs in that relationship and continually provide the attention your friend requires in order to feel healthy and well. It won't occur to you that your empathy for your friend is taking time away from your private life, from your healing time, or from who *you* are as a person and what *you* need. Giving your friends what they need, if you have quite different temperaments, can mean that you're not accepting that you have your own distinct needs.

If you're a highly empathic person, you may not really develop a prioritization for self-acceptance—and you may allow yourself to become unimportant. It's interesting to me that this is something that many spiritual practices teach, and it can be a very significant lesson for some people—but it's sort of overkill for highly empathic people. In many spiritual traditions, especially Buddhism, the idea is to transcend the self, or to release the self and become one with the impermanence. That's a wonderful practice, but I find that highly empathic people tend to do it naturally—they're one with everything *but* themselves. When I ask this sort of person, "What do you want right now?", they'll often have no answer. They may even lack a sense of where their self begins and ends—so self-acceptance for a person who is highly empathic can be a weird nonstarter. There's so much time spent on other people's needs and feelings that their self becomes unimportant. I call these people hyper-empaths, and it's thought that they make up roughly 10 to 15 percent of the population.

When someone says, "This is me—I fit this hyper-empath category. I don't even know what I want in a given situation because I'm so busy attending to everyone else," I explain that the work is to restore their sense of self and to start to understand their own voice, standpoint, and sense of what's true and important for them. That process can begin very simply. People can simply wake up each morning and, while they're still groggy, ask themselves, "What do *I* want to do today?" Certainly, they may need to get ready for work, get the kids up, cook breakfast, and all of sorts of things . . . but when they're still groggy and not fully engaged in the day, and nobody else's needs are in front of them, they can ask, "What do I want to do today?" Then, they should *do* that thing; because it is in doing that thing that they can discover who they truly are. Simply asking about and then meeting their own needs can start people on a path to self-acceptance and self-empathy.

Self-Acceptance and Shame

Another big obstacle to self-acceptance is the beautiful, necessary, and exquisite emotion: shame. Just as we don't tend to think of empathy as a possibly negative thing, we haven't been taught to think of shame as a positive one. That's because many of us know shame as this miserable emotion that can make our lives unrelentingly rotten. However, there's more to shame than that, and it's actually a crucial emotion for self-acceptance—when it's healthy. Shame monitors your behavior: if what you're doing is beneficial; if what you're doing is what you agreed to do; if what you're doing agrees with your moral code; if what you're doing is empathic toward others. Healthy shame asks, "Are you sure you want to say that about her clothes? You might hurt her feelings. You need to be careful." Or, "Are you sure you want that seventh cookie? You probably don't." Those are the kinds of messages you can receive from healthy and authentic shame.

If your shame *isn't* healthy and authentic, however, it can be hypercritical and overbearing. This shame usually doesn't ask you anything—it just yells at you: "Just shut your ignorant mouth! You don't know anything about fashion, you slob." Or, "*You selfish pig!* Your filthy cookie-eating greed is why no one loves you!" Inauthentic and unhealthy shame can be a brutalizing thing that will make self-acceptance unlikely. That sort of shame feels to me like a bad parent, or a bad teacher or coach. It doesn't know how to work with people or how to get things done, so it becomes brutal. Healthy and authentic shame feels like a good parent or teacher, who might gently lean in and ask, "*Really*, are you sure about that? I don't know if you want to do that. Check in with yourself."

The main problem with shame is that many of us learned about shame by *being* shamed. We heard all sorts of unkind and shaming things from parents and other authority figures, many of whom simply didn't know how to work with people. "Don't talk back to me, smarty-pants," or "Hey, you selfish punk, wipe that smile off your face." And those inauthentic and miserable messages are uploaded. A person who doesn't understand the purpose of shame or how to work with it will have only this inauthentic shame that has been placed upon them, rather than a healthy shame that arises authentically and with integrity to help them monitor their own behavior and deal with things that are important to them.

Something important to understand about shame is that it's *supposed* to stop you from doing things, saying things, or moving forward with a possibly bad idea. If you don't know that, you'll tend to think of shame as a controlling, destabilizing mess of an emotion. If you can turn toward shame empathically and understand its actual purpose, you can say, "Oh! This flushing, this inability to speak, this sense of danger almost—this is my shame saying, 'Hold on, buddy. What you're about to do is not right. Stop and drop, pal. Think it over.'" Can you even imagine what a different world we'd have if everyone listened to their healthy shame? Or what Internet commenting would be like if people could just stop for a minute and think before they started typing? Healthy shame is a crucial, beautiful emotion that we haven't been allowed to understand in healthy ways, and that's a real shame.

It's also a shame that self-acceptance is so impeded by unhealthy and inauthentic shame. People who can't accept themselves often need to bring shame out of the shadows and go back to the question for people whose empathy is focused on everyone except them: "What do *I* want to do today?" Then, to access their healthy and authentic shame, they can ask, "What are my morals? What brings me to integrity? What is important to me?" *That's* how to work with shame in a constructive way.

We also need a way to release the inauthentic shaming messages we carry—the ones that were imposed by others. I have an exercise to help people address inauthentic and foreign shame—it's a practice called "Burning Contracts," which helps people separate themselves from behaviors, attitudes, and emotional styles that just aren't working for them. This practice helps people see these behaviors and attitudes as tendencies, and not as concrete facts—and it helps them track back to where their painful and unworkable shame might have come from. It's a tool to figure out, "Is this shame authentic to me? Does it have something important to tell me? Or did I pick it up from someone else?"

If your shame troubles you, you can use this practice to imagine that you have entered into an actual contract with your shameful idea or feeling. For example, your contractual obligation might be for you to repeat: "I'm ten pounds overweight, and that means I'm a worthless failure." When you look at this shaming message through the lens of the Burning Contracts practice, you can separate yourself from the shaming message and see how you react to it now, in this moment. What emotions arise in response to this message? Something *will* arise, because your psyche is constantly working on difficult things, holding on to them, and trying to figure them out!

What I often see is that people can be very cruel to themselves and beat the heck out of themselves in service to an idea that isn't even their own. For instance, it might be that their mother was *extremely* obsessed with weight and they picked up that self-shaming behavior from her. In a way, holding on to that shame is a misguided way of honoring their mother. It's a way of honoring her needs, and saying, "I carry this for you, Mom." I find that many troubling, repetitive, and lingering states have some kind of honor and beauty in them—when you can look at them as contracts you entered into for some important reason.

Instead of always beating yourself up because your shame is acting like a bad coach, you can turn your empathy toward yourself and seek the genius and the honor in what you're doing. With this practice, you can bring sacredness to even your most seemingly unsacred behaviors, and you can discover why your soul has attached itself to the behavior and essentially halted your forward progression as a person. If you can see this halting as a sacred act instead of as a failure, you can discover *why* you have halted and whether you want to stay in that place any longer. You can *decide*. You might even discover that you're working on an issue that goes back in your family or in your culture for generations. If you can approach your contracts as if you're a sociologist or an anthropologist studying your own life, then you may be able to locate yourself in the deeper story of the world instead of just beating yourself up about your weight or whatever it may be for you.

When you can identify your own authentic shame, and when you can make clear separations between your life-giving, necessary shame and the inauthentic shaming messages of others (or your past self), you can identify your own present-day value system. You can also become resilient enough to be able to look at your failings and mistakes without yelling at yourself. Your shame can suddenly become a *good* parent or coach, and you can develop the ability to say to yourself: "Wow that was a mess, what I just did. I need to fix it, apologize, make amends, and learn how to do it better next time."

Notice that this healthy and authentic shame message is focused on what you did. It's not screaming at you and calling you names. It's focusing on the action and what you can do to make amends. This is what healthy and authentic shame should do. It's not entirely *comfortable*—because no one wants to think of themselves as having made mistakes—but it's necessary. It also makes self-acceptance more likely, because even if you screw up, you'll now have your healthy shame helping you so that your screw-ups don't snowball into catastrophes. You can look at yourself and say, "Wow, that was a mess, but I fixed it. Whew! Nice save!"

A sweet thing about healthy shame is that it's never too late to go back and do things right. As you probably know, your shame keeps a tally of the wrongs you've committed. If you understand shame, this tally doesn't have to keep you up at night berating yourself. Instead, you can work hand in hand with your healthy shame, and go back and right those wrongs. It's never too late to say, "You remember six years ago, when I was unkind about that thing you were wearing?" The person might not remember it, but you can say, "You know what? I've felt bad ever since."

Then, you and that person can have a conversation, and you may forge a deeper connection because you were willing to be vulnerable and to call yourself out. Yet, even if the relationship is over, and even if the person never wants to speak to you again, you can always make amends. Sometimes, when things can't be fixed in this world, it's nice to remember that there's another world. It may be time for a grief ritual, an atonement ritual, a shrine, or an altar. You can *always* make amends.

I think part of the reason we have so much trouble with self-acceptance is that we never learn how to empathize and learn from our emotions. Emotions are central to almost everything we think, feel, and do. When we can accept our emotions, then self-acceptance naturally follows. If we *can't* accept our emotions, then it's nearly impossible to accept ourselves, because emotions underlie nearly all of our opinions and most of our actions. Our emotions continually tell us if something feels right or true, or not. They tell us how we feel and who we are. For instance, if we're reading about some political position, our emotions will become involved. We'll get angry: "That's not true!" Maybe we'll be pulled toward that position, and our happiness will arise: "Yes, that's right; that feels right!" It's our emotional response to information—even to mathematics—that tells us what's right. "Two plus two equals . . . " Our emotions tell us that four feels right. "Five? No, it's four. Four feels right."

Emotions and empathy are the foundation of self-awareness, and even though they can impede self-acceptance if we don't understand how they work, they are the foundation of self-acceptance as well. For me, the focus is to empathize with your emotions *and* other people *and* yourself—not one or the other. In that way, you can build an authentic and empathic ground for healthy self-awareness and self-acceptance. It's an emotive and empathic inside job.

4

PERSPECTIVE-TAKING
AS HEALING

Steven C. Hayes

*You can make me hurt, but you cannot make me
turn against my own experience.*

Thank God for panic attacks! Without them, I would have never learned self-acceptance and might have stayed overly interested in objectifying and dehumanizing myself in the interest of achievement. I'm one of the cofounders of Acceptance and Commitment Therapy (ACT), which is an empirically based psychological intervention that combines acceptance and mindfulness strategies with commitment and behavior-change strategies. ACT was born of my own panic disorder.

Panic disorder defines your feeling of anxiety as your enemy, adopts a problem-solving mode of mind toward your own emotions, and threatens you with dire outcomes if you can't eliminate the enemy. You buy into a subtractive idea that when you can diminish or even eliminate your own feelings of vulnerability and anxiety, you'll be able to move forward. For me, my panic disorder reached the point where I could not take a trip, ride in an elevator, sit in a movie theater, go to a restaurant, or give a lecture. (This was especially problematic since I'm a professor.) After three or four years of anxiety struggles, in the winter of 1981–82 when it seemed like my condition was going to destroy everything I cared about, I realized I could no longer run from that monster. I had to turn and walk toward it.

The things I had been doing—medications and traditional cognitive-based therapy—were like pissing into a hurricane. They gave me no traction with which to move forward. So, I went back and drew upon what I had learned as a child of the sixties: spiritual teachings and meditation I practiced while living on an Eastern-focused religious commune, humanistic ideas from the Esalen Institute, est training from the Human Potential Movement, and sitting on Hippie Hill in San Francisco and consuming more chemicals than are probably safe or wise. Inside those experiences was the possibility of looking at myself in a more growth-oriented, holistic way. As I did that, I experienced the traction I was seeking. It gave me the grounding in awareness to examine the thoughts I had that related to panic and to begin to create some distance from them.

There was a key moment in this process. It was the experience of going out of my body and looking at myself *while* I was having a panic attack. If you've ever been in a car accident, you know what I mean—the moment when time slows down and you have a sense that you are watching yourself from the outside. In the middle of this stepping aside from my body, the words that came to me, which I think I actually said out loud, were: "You can make me hurt, but you cannot make me turn against my own experience." The core of this shift in perspective was a change in posture: *I* will *not* run. I am *not* going to run from me.

When I saw this was working for me, I started exploring it and applying it to my psychotherapy with my clients. Sure enough, it had traction for them as well. That led to developing early protocols in the 1980s, testing them, and then working out the basic process and science that led to the first book on ACT in 1999. Now, there are over 145 randomized trials on ACT, thousands of ACT professionals around the world (the Association for Contextual Behavioral Science is the main organization, with nearly 8,000 members), and at least seventy-five professional and self-help books on ACT in dozens of languages.

Perspective-taking, which is at the heart of ACT, taught me a distinct way to approach the challenge of self-acceptance. To do this, we step back just a little bit from our unkind inner voice, notice it as it is, and allow it to say what it says. We listen with a sense of curiosity—acceptance in ACT is not tolerance or resignation, but as if we are receiving a gift. (This is part of the original etymology of the word *acceptance,* and still, in English, when we give a gift we say, "Will you accept this as a token of my appreciation?")

When we've learned what we can from observing our own emotions and thoughts, in ACT we work on attentional flexibility so the voice within can no longer dictate to us and control our life without our will. To do this we use *defusion* methods. *Defusion* is a neologism that means to look at symbolic thought and to notice it as an active mental process, rather than looking at the world that is structured and colored by the lens of thought. Defusion helps undermine experiential avoidance because when we pay attention to the gap between our consciousness (how we are aware of thoughts) and the content of thoughts we have the capacity to choose. Employing defusion, we can more easily shift toward what we care about most deeply, taking what's useful and leaving worry, fear, judgment, and self-loathing behind.

For example, consider someone who is working with a body image challenge. I'd encourage them first to just listen to their inner voice. It may be saying things that could be useful, such as warnings that they've put on too many pounds and should exercise for the sake of their health. There may also be not-so-useful pieces, like the idea that they're ugly, unlovable, or unacceptable—that there's something wrong with them. I'd encourage them to back up and try to listen to that unkind voice with a sense of kindness and self-compassion. Often, the seeds of our self-doubts, shame, and self-criticism were planted in childhood. I would ask them to picture themselves as a child saying things like "I'm ugly. I'm unlovable." Then I'd ask them what they would do if a child shared such self-judgments. They probably wouldn't slap that child, criticize her, or tell her to snap out of it! Instead, they'd probably listen, embrace the child, and help her step forward even with her fears. Well, why should the grown-up deserve anything less?

There are myriad defusion methods—the ACT community is inventing them all the time. One might distill the self-judgment down to a single word and then repeat it aloud. For example: *Ugly. Ugly. Ugly.* The person suffering with poor body image would say this rapidly for thirty seconds. They might sing a song of "I'm ugly" or "I'm unlovable" to the tune of "Happy Birthday," or say it in a silly voice. Our research has shown that such methods quickly reduce the distress of such judgments and undermine their believability as their literal meaning drops away. Those are the common outcomes of cognitive defusion, but it occurs without cognitive challenge or disputation.

Another defusion method that can create a sense of distance might be to repeat, "I'm having the *thought* that I'm ugly; I'm having the *thought* that I'm unlovable." By labeling the thought, we take a compassionate, gentle, and loving stance with ourselves, just as we might with a child who has declared, "I'm unlovable." That place of perspective-taking and self-compassion opens up very naturally when we begin to see language in flight and no longer see the world through a lens of judgmental language. We have to be careful to avoid self-ridicule when using defusion methods, because defusion is not ridiculous. There's a certain bittersweet quality to seeing how our minds work—it's very human—so even the more humorous defusion methods are not meant to be a new way to mock, shame, or blame oneself.

Defusion techniques liberate us and take us from the limitations that happen with automatic and problem-solving modes of mind—there is a space that opens up with a more aware, descriptive mind. I like to call it the *sunset mode*. When we look at a sunset we don't say, "Oh, gee . . . you know, that pink is a little off and the blue could be brighter." If we can bring that sunset mode of mind to our difficult self-judgmental thoughts, we find that we have more flexibility than when arguing with ourselves about them, trying to convince ourselves we're wrong, or worse, criticizing ourselves for having the thought in the first place when we probably came to it honestly through the media or our families.

Here's an exercise that can help you learn to practice perspective-taking:

- Close your eyes and get in contact with whatever you're struggling with. Take some time to feel what you feel, think what you think, and remember what you remember. Don't try to fix it; try to contact your own suffering.

- As you do that, notice that there's a part of you noticing that suffering. Awareness resides—catch the *fromness* of consciousness, not consciousness *of* sometime.

- Take that noticing part of pure awareness and imagine leaving your body and looking back at yourself. Notice what you look like when you are suffering.

- Ask yourself (but do not answer . . . just hold the question in, in awareness): "What do you think of that person? Is this a lovable person? Is it a whole person?"

- Send that point of consciousness to the other side of the room, leaving yourself sitting there. Now look back at yourself from afar. See yourself sitting there, suffering. You might notice that there are other people not too far away—in your house or neighborhood—who are suffering as well.

- Ask yourself again (but do not answer . . . just hold the question in, in awareness): "What do you think of that person? Is this a lovable person? Is he or she a whole person?"

- As you picture yourself from across the room, imagine this is a memory. You remember reading a book that asked you to look at yourself from across the room while feeling this event that was causing suffering. But it is ten years from now and you have grown far wiser. Look at yourself sitting there ten years ago. If you could pass back two or three sentences from a wiser future, what would you pass back to yourself?

• Sit with that for a few moments, and then write yourself a short note of advice.

• Then bring yourself back into your present, into your body. Consider what you wrote on the note. See if it gives you a place to go.

Here's the point to this exercise. Perspective-taking is at the core of human consciousness. It includes person, place, and time—the three relations I just played with in this exercise. My guess is that the note you wrote was kind, accepting, and encouraging. Human conscious-ness is like that—inherently self-compassionate and compassionate toward others. The world's spiritual traditions that have been teaching us for millennia that through contemplative practice we can create a different mode of mind and a different world are exactly right. From an ACT point of view, we have good reason to believe that this simple perspective-taking between speakers and listeners as a form of coop-eration (called Relational Frame Theory) evolved with language, about 100,000 to perhaps 400,000 years ago.

There's a form of perspective-taking when we know a name for an object—we know it means we should orient toward the object when we hear the name. Twelve-month-old babies will do that—it's a very basic process. Nonhuman animals do not, not even the language-trained chimps. This ability to see relations from both sides (object → name implied name → object) is at the core of human cognition. It initially just allowed us to be more cooperative—I could call across a ravine for an apple and know my tribe-mate would look for one—but it soon extended to all cognitive relations and helped humans break free from the physical properties of events. A nickel is bigger than a dime to a three-year-old, but when we learn comparative relations as a kind of arbitrary perspective-taking (from the point of view of a nickel, a dime is larger), then a dime can be bigger than a nickel to a six-year-old even without having experiences with dimes. This is a wonderful ability—it allows us to arbitrarily compare things, to imagine futures that have never been, and to pick among the imagined consequences of alternative courses of action. But this same set of cognitive abilities that allows us to verbally solve problems allows us to reflect back on ourselves and think of our life as a problem to be solved. We started chopping ourselves up and saying, "I like this . . . I don't like this . . . I want this . . . I don't want this." Moreover, many things we like, want, or don't want are things that are part of our history, and they have no place else to go. We can't slice and dice ourselves in that way.

Getting back to perspective-taking helps with taking this problem-solving mode of mind and moving it into a more descriptive and appreciative mode that is closer to where language began. It gives us a way of seeing ourselves as whole, watching these mental processes, and allowing them to just be. We shift away from the subtractive, limited, judgmental mode of mind of "I want this . . . I don't want this . . . " which is good for problem solving but dangerous when applied within. That's why we need to back off and embrace the whole of who we are, and perspective-taking will help do that. Putting language on a leash and learning how to use our different modes of mind is the ACT way of taking the spiritual/mindfulness traditions and bringing them to Western science, not out of sacrilege, but to simplify a way of approaching our problems.

Once we are in a more self-compassionate mode of mind, it is natural to treat our experiences with greater self-kindness. Emotions are designed to be felt, but not felt constantly and ruminatively. Take shame for example. Shame includes an element that's actually good for us: guilt. Guilt is useful, but the thought—"I'm bad"—that combines with guilt to produce shame is usually not so useful. This returns us to defusion. When we use defusion to back up and watch that categorical judgment arise and have a little bit of separation from it, then what's left is the feeling of sadness, and of loss, and of loss of potential that can inform, vitalize, and enable us to walk a sometimes difficult path.

Take addiction work—shame correlates negatively with addiction treatment; but guilt correlates positively. We recently published a randomized trial on a treatment for shame and substance abuse adding six hours of ACT to a twenty-eight-day, twelve-step-oriented inpatient program (Luoma, Kohlenberg, Hayes, & Fletcher, 2012). Post-treatment, our outcomes were worse than the program as it was, but by follow-up, the outcomes were much better. That is because shame came down quickly in the twelve-step program, but it soon rebounded back to baseline because it was done suppressively, sort of like the Stuart Smalley character on *Saturday Night Live*. With a little help in defusion, acceptance, and perspective-taking from the ACT groups, real healing happened. It happened more slowly, but it continued to occur. What that tells me is people can try to deal with their emotions in a way that looks healthy but is not—they'll neglect the deep exploration into the source of the pain and the challenging task of changing their relationship with self-judgment.

One of our clients in an early trial of ACT for substance use had been high on heroin while his daughter was being abused in the back bedroom, and he didn't get up and do anything about it. He had a lot of pain to feel. These kinds of things can't be sorted out in a twenty-eight-day intake program. So we walked him into the memories. We walked him into how his body responded. We walked him into noticing what his mind does with it and how it tries to judge him and push him to do more of the same because there was something wrong with him. Then we helped him find the courage to stand with himself as a whole human being, taking responsibility for the things that he'd done, and allowing those feelings to motivate him to reach out and be the best parent and the best person he could be. The shift toward values and valued living, which is key in an ACT approach, is fostered by this embrace of emotion and experience—including ones that nominally are considered negative. They're negative only in the sense that they are painful, but many emotions are both painful and useful.

If you look at a child you love, you can feel a bittersweet quality of the fear you have for how things will go for them, and the knowledge that they will die someday, and the potential for them to come to harm. These are not negative things to be erased or eliminated—any good parent knows that. That sense of vulnerability handled well is part of being a good parent, part of being loving toward your kids. If you walk through that in every area of your life where anxiety, sadness, and grief reside within you, there is a link to what you care about. Teaching people to go into that place, to feel it on purpose, to feel it as it is—as they might reach out and feel a table—is something that most people don't get much training in. When they do, it empowers them to be able to shift toward what they deeply care about and link their behavior to it.

That's part of liberation; that's part of human empowerment that gets missed in our avoidant culture that teaches us that the right car, the right spouse, the right beer, the right house, the right sum of money is going to somehow create a life worth living. That's a lie—it's always been a lie—but we're often unlikely in this society to actually challenge it.

This brings me to the "C" in ACT—commitment. Commitment means embracing our capacity to choose our values. By values, I'm not referring to the things we use to evaluate ourselves. I don't mean goals or judgments. I mean the chosen qualities of being and doing that bring vitality, meaning, and purpose in the moment. They are never final—they're part of the journey.

That commitment is the commitment to be true to yourself, to have your moments on Earth be about building a larger pattern of values-based action so that your habits of mind become your friend instead of your enemy. As you practice self-acceptance, compassion toward others, and wholeness, your contribution, participation, play, and relationships begin to line up with your purposes. That beginning is up to you, the person in the mirror. We know that the kinds of values that build commitment are not the ones that have the word *should* in them. They don't include *have to* or *must*. They're things that feel intrinsic and freely chosen. If you link your behavior to qualities that you choose freely, and build larger and larger life patterns around that, life will lift you up and you can carry the pain, disappointments, and mistakes forward. This will help you in your journey because the places where you hurt are the places where you care. Conversely, if you're not willing to hurt, you can't afford to care.

For example, if you've been betrayed in love—and almost all of us have—your mind is going to tell you to protect yourself against future pain by never being so vulnerable and open and intimate again. You're not going to be able to go back to innocence—and that's a good thing because ignorance is *not* bliss; it is ignorance. Your mind tries to protect you from hurt by essentially eliminating your caring, and so you start detuning relationships. If a new relationship shows up that really could touch you deeply, you know that openness to wounding will come with that. As that door opens up, you can feel part of you wanting to run away, wanting to somehow mess up the relationship. What you have to do is find the place where you can be more open to pain and step forward as a kind of act of faith in yourself. To be okay about being close to others means being okay about the possibility of being hurt. If you form an intimate relationship, even if you never deliberately hurt each other, one of you is going to die first, and you think you're not going to feel left behind or betrayed? Think again.

Hurt, pain, loss, and finitude are part of life itself, and there's a natural link between the one side of the coin that says "pain" and the other side of the coin that says "caring." Human consciousness and perspective-taking are the keys to being able to have both. This model applies to every area that matters to us. It is not a matter of tolerance and resignation. When we receive the gift of what's inside our pain, we can move our attention toward what we deeply care about and commit our life to that without having to hide from our own pain and finitude. We no longer have to hide from the fact that love includes loss, or that life includes death.

5

EMBRACING ALL OF OUR PARTS

Jay Earley

*Self-acceptance is the ability to accept all of our parts
and to be open to them, even interested in them.*

Most people begin therapy because they're unhappy with something in their lives. Maybe they procrastinate too much, they get too angry, they feel bad about themselves, or they're scared to move forward. All of these are, of course, the opposite of self-acceptance.

I practice Internal Family Systems (IFS) therapy—which is a form of individual therapy created by Richard Schwartz. IFS works with the *parts* of us, or our sub-personalities. It provides wonderful ways to understand and implement self-acceptance. What I've learned from practicing IFS is that whenever somebody has a psychological problem, it's because some part of them is causing the issue. Using the IFS model, self-acceptance is the ability to accept all of your parts and to be open to them, even interested in them. IFS works with our parts—the part of me that procrastinates, the part of me that gets angry, or tries to please people, for example. You may not like a part that feels bad about yourself or that is scared to move ahead, but once you get to know each part and find out what it's actually trying to do for you, it's easier to accept it.

The beautiful thing that I've discovered using IFS is that all of our parts have a positive intent for us. For example, if you have a part that causes you to procrastinate and avoid doing things that you need to do, this causes problems. That part may not be playing a positive role, but it's trying to. Perhaps that part is afraid that if it lets you go ahead and do a task that you're trying to do, you're going to fail, or get judged or shamed, and feel bad about yourself. So this procrastinating part is saying, "Let's not do it. Let's avoid this because I want to keep you from failing and feeling bad." That's not a viable strategy, but the part's intention is a positive one. It's trying to protect you from pain. Of course, it may actually be causing you even more pain in the process, but it doesn't know that. All it knows is: risks are dangerous, don't go there, and don't try to do that task. That's an example of a part having a positive intent even if its effect is negative.

It's helpful to think of the parts like little people inside us with their own motivations and fears—even their own memories. I actually think that is the way the psyche is structured, but I can't prove it. What I *do* know is that if you treat your parts as if they are little people you can talk to, the parts respond in a very positive way. In fact, you might even hear a part say, "Thank you! You're finally paying attention to me after all these years." Working with parts is very powerful because it gives you extensive contact with the different areas of your psyche, and tremendous power to change things.

From my own experience in working on myself and working with many clients over the years, I've seen that the parts really seem to have their own little psychological lives. One of the most important aspects of IFS is developing a relationship with each of these parts. These parts act like people. They have feelings and reactions.

You go inside and feel a part in your body or get an image of what it looks like. Then you ask the part questions silently and listen for its responses. It will tell you what it is trying to do for you or what pain it is trying to protect you from. In addition, a part might say that it doesn't trust you because you haven't helped in the past. Some parts will say they've been longing to have you finally appreciate them, and they feel wonderful when you do. When that happens, the experience is not just getting insight into a psychological issue in your head—you are actually talking to a little being inside you, and it has its own feelings.

The Inner Critic is the type of part that keeps us from accepting ourselves. Most people have more than one part that's an Inner Critic. Even though we often think of *the* Inner Critic, when you actually use IFS to look inside the psyche, you realize that there is more than one self-critical part. Here's an example that comes up frequently: you'll have a part that tells you, "Oh, you can't do that. You're not going to be successful. If you try to do that, you're going to fail. Don't bother." That's a typical Inner Critic attack.

As another example, suppose you have a part that says, "You are lazy; you're not working hard enough. What's the matter with you? You should do that . . . but I know you can't." That's another typical Inner Critic message. When you get to know an Inner Critic part, it might tell you, "I'm doing this because I'm trying to get you to work hard, so you'll do things well so you won't get criticized." Now, of course, the part is criticizing you, but it is trying to protect you from what it perceives as danger or pain.

Perhaps that Inner Critic is attempting to protect you from a critical parent. You might think this is just an internalization of the critical parent, but it's actually more than that. The part is actually trying to protect you by pushing you to be successful so your parent *won't* criticize you. Of course, it doesn't work that way—a part like that usually *prevents* you from being successful because of its judgments, but the part doesn't realize that. It's doing what it can to protect you from what it believes will be intolerable suffering.

We don't just listen for and notice our parts' voices. We actually go inside, find out exactly which part is speaking, and then have a dialogue with the part. IFS clients learn to differentiate one part from another—not just critical parts, but all parts. When you talk to your parts, you're not just working with a theory about your psychodynamics, you are making contact with what's there.

In IFS, the Inner Critic parts are types of parts known as *protectors*. There are many kinds of protectors. Many result from childhood situations where you were hurt or neglected, and as a result, you have a young child part that's in a lot of pain. A protector arises to try to protect you from being overwhelmed by that pain. Alternatively, if you were harmed as a child, then a protector may arise to try to prevent the harm from happening again or stop it when it does.

The parts that carry this underlying pain from childhood are called *exiles* in IFS. Exiles are parts that hold pain from traumatic incidents or harmful or neglectful relationships. These relationships usually (but not always) occur in childhood.

This brings us to the capital "S" Self. In IFS, in addition to all of your parts—the protectors and the exiles—there is the *Self*, which is who we truly are when none of our parts is dominant. It's actually not that hard for most people to access their Self. It is a place of compassion for and curiosity about your parts, a place of connection and calm, and most importantly, a place of self-acceptance. By accessing your Self and getting to know each of your parts, you can find out what each part is trying to do for you from its own (often distorted) perspective, and then accept that part and make a connection with it. This leads to *transformation*, which is the goal of IFS therapy.

There are a number of different ways to recognize your Self. Richard Schwartz, the founding developer of IFS, discovered that when he was working with his clients, occasionally a client would say, "It feels like I'm not in a part right now; it feels like this is *who I really am*. I feel open and I feel compassionate." When we connect to our true Self, there is a different internal sense—a sense of being home, a sense of being open. It's similar to the place you get into when you meditate, but in IFS you can determine whether you're in Self by noticing how you feel toward the part you are working on. If you feel interested in the part and openly curious about it or compassionate toward it, then you're in Self. If you feel judgmental or have thoughts like, "I hate this part. I want to get rid of it. It's causing me problems," then you're not in Self; you're in a part (a different part).

The Self is naturally interested in connecting with all of our parts. When you're in Self, you're accepting and compassionate about the pain that your exiles carry and the pain your protectors are trying to avoid. When you're in Self, it's easy to focus on a particular protector and get to know it and find out what it's trying to do for you.

This includes the Inner Critic. Paradoxically, even though the Inner Critic parts don't accept us, we can accept them. When we do so and then follow through with the rest of the IFS process, the Inner Critic parts can actually be transformed from their dysfunctional role of criticizing us. They can choose a healthier role—for example, being there in a constructive, encouraging way to help us see what we need to look at and grow.

Sometimes a transformed Inner Critic will take an entirely different role. A part may say to you, "You shouldn't have eaten that. Why did you eat that? You were on a diet and you've blown it!" You start by getting into Self and asking the part questions and finding out what it's trying to do for you by criticizing you in that way. And, of course, in this case, its positive intent is pretty easy to see: this part is trying to keep you on a diet so you will be healthy or lose weight. Now, of course, this Inner Critic is going to be at war with another part that tends to overeat. The beautiful thing about IFS is that the Self can get to know and accept both parts and find out what they are trying to do for you.

So let's say you are working on that Inner Critic part that's bashing you because you overate. You ask yourself, "What is my attitude toward this critical part?" Perhaps you wish it would go away because you don't like it. If that's your attitude, it's not coming from Self. It's coming from a part that doesn't like the Inner Critic. You ask that other part, which I call the Inner Defender, if it would be willing to step aside just for the rest of the therapy session so that you can get to know this Inner Critic from an open place. You might even explain to the Inner Defender, "If you're willing to step aside and let me get to know the Critic, then I can help to transform it." In this way, the Inner Defender is motivated to step aside. If there's more than one part that doesn't like the Inner Critic, you might have to ask a couple of them to step aside.

Once they do, you're in Self, because the Self is who you truly are. You don't have to manufacture the Self. All you have to do is get the parts that are activated at any given time to step aside, and then you are naturally in Self. Look at it from a spiritual perspective. How many spiritual traditions say that love is what everything is really made of? This is because love is who we are—and the Self is love.

To get to that place of Self-love and transformation, you begin by working with the protector you have chosen to focus on. You develop a relationship between your Self and the protector where the protector trusts you. Then, you ask the protector to give you permission to work with the exile it's protecting. One of the things that makes IFS so powerful, as opposed to other forms of therapy, is that you don't just dive into the exiles—the child parts that are in pain; you ask permission from the protectors first. That way they're not going to keep sabotaging your work.

Once you get permission from your protectors, you get to know the exile, find out what pain it's in, and ask it to show you what happened when you were young to cause it that pain. Then, from Self you witness the pain the exile went through so that it really feels understood by you. That opens up the exile for healing. You follow this with three additional healing steps:

1. *Reparenting.* As Self, you enter that scene in the past and give the exile what it needed back then, or protect it from whatever harm was caused.

2. *Retrieval.* You take the exile out of that past situation and bring it into your current life, or into your heart, or into some lovely place where it can be safe and comfortable and be with you.

3. *Unburdening.* You do an internal unburdening ritual where you help the exile to release the burdens—the pain and the negative beliefs from childhood—that it's been carrying.

Once an exile lets go of its burdens, it assumes its natural state of being loving, playful, creative, strong, or whatever. When the protector sees that the exile is no longer in danger or in pain, it will realize that it doesn't have to play its role anymore. So you go back to the protector and say, "Do you see that the exile has been transformed? Can you now let go of your protective role?" The protector can now opt for a different role in your psyche if it likes.

For example, if you're working with an Inner Critic part, that Inner Critic part might choose to become what we call an Inner Mentor. Instead of criticizing you, it might choose to help you look at the ways you need to improve. This is what the critic was trying to do, but it was doing it in a harmful way, whereas the Inner Mentor will do it in a supportive, caring, and encouraging way. We don't assign the Inner Critic its new role; the Inner Critic chooses what it wants to do.

Because of IFS, the exiles and the protectors transform into healthy roles and come to trust the Self. The Self is the natural leader for the internal family system. Once you have transformed many of your parts, they will still be there, but now they can offer you their positive qualities or capabilities. They will also work together with the Self and each other, so that the Self decides what needs to happen in any given moment and brings in the part that is needed. When you transform your Inner Critics, you automatically become self-accepting because you are no longer judging or pushing yourself. When you are in Self, you naturally accept and love yourself because that is your true nature.

6

MOVING TOWARD
A WISE MIND VIEW

Erin Olivo

*Our sense of self-worth is much less easily shaken
if it is derived from a deeply held sense of self-
compassion and self-respect, rather than being
contingent on fulfilling certain ideals.*

As a clinical psychologist for the past twenty years, I work directly with patients who suffer from different kinds of emotional challenges and often engage in self-destructive behaviors. Many of my patients have been diagnosed with depression and anxiety, and they struggle with addiction, overeating, and other forms of self-sabotage. For most, these destructive behaviors represent their best attempts at managing distressing emotions, but there is often a core underlying feeling of unworthiness and self-loathing. In order for my patients to break free of these patterns, they need to learn to regulate their emotions and behaviors, as well as become more kind and compassionate toward themselves. The psychotherapy approach I use to help them with this is mindfulness based and employs elements of cognitive behavior therapy (CBT) and dialectical behavior therapy (DBT). I teach my patients a set of strategies focused on helping them achieve a more balanced approach to life—a philosophy I call *Wise Mind Living*.

Before I go into more detail about my approach to helping people, I think it is important to make a distinction between self-esteem and self-acceptance. As I see it, the goal of self-acceptance work isn't to make people feel good about themselves all the time, or to merely boost their self-esteem. I don't believe that is realistic, and studies indicate it isn't likely to change peoples' lives all that much. In fact, research shows that interventions focused specifically on boosting self-esteem are not very effective at reducing conditions like depression and anxiety in the long term. By contrast, interventions that are focused on cultivating self-compassion are far more effective in these areas. In addition, research shows that people with higher levels of self-compassion have steadier and more constant feelings of self-worth than people who simply score high on self-esteem. Lastly, research reveals that self-compassion is far less likely than self-esteem to be contingent on specific factors like social approval, competing successfully, or feeling attractive. In other words, our sense of self-worth is much less easily shaken if it is derived from a deeply held sense of self-compassion and self-respect, rather than being contingent on fulfilling certain ideals.

Instead of simply focusing on improving self-esteem, I work with my patients to cultivate a more accepting, Wise Mind view of themselves. That means compassionately knowing and accepting yourself for *all* of who you are—the good, the bad, and everything in between. It means working on acknowledging and forgiving yourself for your shortcomings. It also means becoming aware of when your negative view of yourself might actually be distorted or flat-out wrong. Some of the strategies I teach my patients to help them cultivate Wise Mind self view are: *Mindfulness of the States of Mind, Mindfulness of the Cycle of Emotion, Identifying and Challenging Negative Self-Talk,* and *Acceptance Strategies.*

States of Mind

The very first thing I teach my patients is how to identify the three main states of mind that we all live in:

- Emotion Mind
- Logic Mind
- Wise Mind

Emotion Mind is when our thinking and behavior are driven by our emotions in the moment. The polar opposite of that is Logic Mind, a purely rational state that gives absolutely no consideration to the emotional aspect of how we feel about something. Wise Mind is the synthesis of Emotion Mind and Logic Mind. It is exactly what it sounds like: a state of mind where you have a logical perspective, but can also acknowledge and appreciate the emotional aspects of a situation.

The good news is that when we are stuck in Emotion Mind we can move toward Wise Mind by using mindfulness and emotion-regulation strategies. First, we need to calm down our body so our brain can work more clearly, because emotions create a physiological response that disrupts clear thinking. We all know those sensations we experience when we're in Emotion Mind—our heart starts to pound, and we feel hot, shaky, and a little nauseated. On the other hand, we may feel energized, tense, and ready to jump. Either way, there's something going on in the body that prevents our brain from thinking rationally or from keeping things in perspective. I begin by teaching my patients exercises such as rhythmic breathing, progressive muscle relaxation, and visualization techniques designed to help them calm down their overheated physical states.

The Cycle of Emotion

The next group of strategies I teach my patients involves learning to identify and be more mindful of their emotions and what triggers them. We begin by cultivating mindful awareness of the internal cycle of emotion that includes thoughts, physical feelings, impulses, and behavioral actions. Often, as my patients begin to mindfully observe their distressing emotions and behaviors, they find that at the root of each cycle is a pervasive *core* sense of unworthiness that often acts as a filter through which they view themselves, others, and their world in general.

Patients discover that this cycle often begins when negative self-talk or their lack of self-acceptance leads to a distressing emotion, which in turn changes how they feel in their body, which then triggers an urge to engage in destructive behavior. This tends to generate even more negative emotion and negative self-talk—and the cycle continues. Learning to slow down and be mindful of this cycle is the first step toward being able to change how we feel. Indeed, sometimes that's all it takes to shift an emotional experience, although it's important to take the next step and begin working with the information that has been uncovered.

Identifying and Challenging Negative Self-Talk

Once my patients have identified the cycle of emotion and gained more awareness of the story they are telling themselves about a situation, they can begin to challenge the way they are thinking. This involves looking for the facts in a situation, rather than just succumbing to opinions and what I call *hot thoughts*—which support a specific feeling. To move into a more fact-based point of view requires actively seeking evidence to challenge the thoughts one is having.

Imagine you are a student who just took a test, and you are feeling anxious about how you did. Before you even get your results, you decide you've done horribly. This leads you to conclude that, in fact, you must be stupid, and you begin to worry that you're going to fail out of school, which in turn leads to feelings of total despair. Such feelings may then trigger an urge to use food, alcohol, or drugs as an escape. Keep in mind, this all started with nothing more than a bad feeling about a test, without any supporting evidence.

In such a situation, I would ask a patient to stop and write down all of these hot thoughts. I would ask them to go through each statement and challenge the validity of every one using factual evidence. Starting with the first statement, "I know I failed," I might ask: "How do you know you failed? You don't have the score yet. Where's the evidence for that?" Then on to the next thought: "Does doing badly on one test really indicate that someone is stupid? Could that perhaps be an unfair label?" and "Would you really get kicked out of school for doing poorly on one test?"

When doing this type of thought-challenge exercise, I insist that patients stick with the facts. I ask them to imagine themselves presenting their case before a judge in a court of law, where a person cannot be condemned based on possibilities, hunches, opinions, or fearful predictions.

The example I've used is based on one of my patients who went through this exact experience. Guess what? She got an A on the test! Furthermore, when we were going through this thought-challenge process, she realized, "These are the thoughts I have *every* time I take a test, even though I've never actually failed!" She learned that when something is important to her and she is worried about succeeding, her mind habitually goes to a place of negative predictions and self-criticism.

The good news is that the more we do these thought-challenging exercises, the easier it becomes to recognize such negative patterns of thinking. With time and practice—while we may still have the negative thought—we will quickly be able to recognize it for what it is: "Oh, this is my racket—this is the thing I tell myself when I'm really afraid, or when I'm really worried."

Sometimes we might indeed fail the test, do something wrong, or behave in a destructive way. What then? We also need strategies to help us cope with bad situations without being self-destructive—strategies such as acceptance and forgiveness.

Balancing Change-Oriented Strategies with Acceptance Strategies

As I have mentioned, I use a psychological approach called dialectical behavior therapy (DBT), and the hallmark of this approach is the use of the seemingly opposite ideas (the dialectic) of acceptance and change. This means that while many of the methods (like the thought-challenge strategy I discussed earlier) are focused on changing the way a patient thinks or behaves, I simultaneously teach strategies focused on helping patients to validate and accept themselves, no matter how they might be struggling.

My patients often don't understand what in the world could be good about validating or accepting the things they don't like about themselves. They worry that if they accept themselves, the things they don't like will just become worse. They say things like, "I can't validate this. I have to beat myself up about it or else I'll never change it."

Take addiction, for example. A patient might come to me and say, "I am in self-loathing about the fact that I continue to drink. I know that my drinking is destructive, but I can't do anything about it, and I hate myself for it." I start by reminding them that self-loathing is putting them in Emotion Mind, and when they're in Emotion Mind they are much less able to change any of the destructive behaviors they're engaging in. Self-criticism and judgment perpetuate the negative cycle of emotion and behavior.

One of the keys to breaking this destructive cycle is to practice acceptance. Because there are so many misconceptions about this very abstract idea, I think it's important to clarify exactly what acceptance is, and what it *isn't*. Acceptance does not mean: "I like this." Acceptance does not mean: "I'm *never* going to change this." Acceptance means acknowledging what is happening in the present moment and allowing it to be as it is, without fighting reality.

Acceptance is the first step toward cultivating forgiveness and understanding, but it's also the first step toward effecting change. By acknowledging and accepting that we are doing the best we can right now *and* that we would like to do better, we can begin (without judgment or shame) to set personal goals and work toward them.

I regularly ask my patients to practice an exercise that helps them cultivate self-compassion. Similar to a loving-kindness meditation, this involves picturing someone who is struggling with an issue similar to the one the patient is facing. It can be a real or imagined person, but the aim is to choose someone the patient can identify with and whose situation is familiar. I then ask my patient whether they feel they could forgive, accept, or have compassion for this person. Tapping into their innate human empathy, they usually say, "Of course I can feel compassion for this person. I completely understand why they are struggling. Look at the life they've had and the challenges they've faced. They deserve my compassion." I ask them to take a moment to imagine sharing this acceptance and compassion with the other person. Then, I ask them to redirect that same sentiment toward themselves by envisioning that they are sitting across from a childhood version of themselves. I ask them to offer that love, compassion, and forgiveness to the child who will grow up to be the person they are today. Finally, I ask them to envision increasingly older versions of themselves until they are offering acceptance and compassion to their present-day self.

The Wise Mind View

Cultivating a more compassionate Wise Mind view of oneself requires a commitment to introspective work that focuses in equal parts on change and acceptance. Sometimes this can be challenging, but it's essential that we pursue our goals with compassion, and that the change we seek in ourselves does not overshadow or undermine our sense of self-acceptance. Self-acceptance cannot be conditional. Self-acceptance is based in the here-and-now; it is not future-oriented. If we find ourselves saying, "I'll be okay when . . . " or "I only deserve it if . . . ", that is not self-acceptance. Wise Mind knows we are a work in progress, we are doing the best that we can, and that, with compassionate support, we can grow into the person we want to be.

7

CURIOSITY IS THE KEY

Harville Hendrix & Helen LaKelly Hunt

Someone who is able to fully let in love is someone who is willing to live in the mystery of who they are.

We often write about a concept that we've developed called *zero negativity*, or ZN, in relationships. When one decides to go ZN, they relinquish all transactions that "put down" their partner. Examples include rolling your eyes, frowning, or saying, "Where did that come from?" in a pejorative tone. All these interactions devalue or make another person bad, in some way. ZN includes surrendering negative references to one's self, also. ZN is both implicit and explicit in most of the spiritual practices and traditions of the world. Simply sitting in meditation and watching our thoughts arise and learning to release them without judgment—letting them go—that's a part of moving toward a relational zero negativity. It's about being in a relationship *to the self* in zero negativity.

Most people experience moments of self-criticism—real harshness toward themselves—so to move in the direction of self-acceptance from a cognitive perspective is to consider and process what the function of the negativity is. Everything we do serves a function for our psychic economy. For example, when you think of ZN as a "put down" of others, it may compensate for our low self-esteem or be an attempt to take charge and be in control by devaluing how someone else is doing something. No behavior occurs without an intention, even when the behavior looks erratic, chaotic, or random. All behavior prevents something fearful from happening, which we think would happen without that behavior. There is always some causality, whatever we do, although the cause may be out of our awareness.

For example, we met a person who was working on their doctoral dissertation. The dissertation had been ready for submission for about three months, and everybody around the graduate student was providing an enormous amount of positive appreciation for the dissertation. Nevertheless, this student kept saying, "It's not good enough. It's not good enough." When we finally asked, "What's the function of 'It's not good enough' for you?", the answer came quickly.

For the student, the function of the self put-down was that if they told themselves, "It's not good enough," and "I'm not good enough," and "I'm not smart enough," they would prevent themselves from experiencing a relational transaction with their professor in which their fears might come true. Therefore, the function of the negativity was to prevent something from happening that in their anticipation and in their imagination was worse than not turning in the doctoral dissertation.

Then we asked, "Where do you think this process comes from? Where does the self put-down come from?" The student, like most people, could trace it back to something that happened earlier in life. There is always trauma behind any negative self-belief that comes up. What is interesting is that the self-belief serves the psychic economy by *preventing* something from happening. If it happened, we think it would be worse than turning a dissertation in or whatever outcome we're dreading. In other words, the anticipatory rejection would come true.

When people find themselves in situations like this, where they feel beset by self-judgment or criticism, we recommend two actions: The first is an exploration of the self—where does this idea come from? How old is it? What is it related to? What is it protecting you from if you don't act? The second action is to accept the positive data.

We have a personal story about this from when I (Harville) was in my forties (which is now a long time ago) during the early stages of developing Imago theory. When I refer to Imago, I'm referring to a couples' therapy Helen and I co-created, starting in the late 1970s. I was beginning to lecture publicly and became aware that every time I was on my way to a speaking engagement the armpits of my jacket—I wore a jacket and tie in those days—were soggy wet.

I decided to examine this and asked myself, "What am I imagining is going to happen when I walk on that stage and pick up that microphone?" It took a while to get to it, but my fantasy was that somebody in the audience would be smarter than I was, would see me as saying stuff that I couldn't defend or didn't have any research behind. I would be humiliated and shamed. I had to explore my response to myself and get clear about what was going on.

The next time I was scheduled to give a lecture, I changed my outcome picture. I envisioned people applauding me when I walked onstage and giving me a standing ovation when I'd finished speaking. I held that image in my mind during a thirty-five-minute drive to a speaking event. I noticed as I was driving I'd stopped perspiring, and then, once I'd given the lecture, I got a standing ovation!

After that, I began to accumulate data. I had been making myself terrified, so I said to myself, "I'm an expert on Imago. I know more about this topic than anyone else in the world because Helen and I made up the theory. I am a co-creator of this. There may be other theories, but nobody can cross me up on this one. They can say it's wrong, but they can't say that it's illogical or irrational, because I know what it is."

The process wasn't instantaneous. I was still aware that there was a part of me that didn't think I was that smart, although I was not as anxious about it. Once the book *Getting the Love You Want* came out, the huge response shocked both of us. I became aware of a collapse in my mental construct of "I'm not that smart." It was clear that if I were not smart, people would not have responded with the enthusiasm and in the numbers they had.

That was how I explored and accepted my data. *Where does it come from? What is the catastrophic imagination in terms of the outcome? What is the real data?* In our workshops, Helen talks about the neuroscience of the brain: she talks about the necessity of moving from the limbic system into the cortical system and processing the data that is entering. It is a way of using the thinking process, the cortical brain, to begin to regulate the limbic brain and begin to assimilate the data that is contrary to the actual situation.

The limbic brain is where our feelings and the neuro-mechanisms that sense safety or danger in our environment reside. It is where the amygdala is housed, and the amygdala is constantly looking for the bad stuff that's going to happen or might happen. When there *is* some sense that something bad could happen, or is happening, there is a neuro-chemical response because of the signal coming from the limbic system that something is dangerous in the environment. The neurochemical element of that is cortisol. When cortisol enters the bloodstream, it is triggered by a fear response. Cortisol then permeates our sensory system, and we begin to feel like we are in a dangerous environment. It takes some of us a long time to metabolize that. Usually, we can only metabolize it if nothing bad actually does happen and/or if something positive does happen.

This neurochemical connection between our ability to be kind and loving toward ourselves and the quality of our intimate relationships is a one-to-one correlation. The reason is that reality is relationship; reality is connecting. We are part of a network, and that network is our context.

Since the 1970s, with the popularization by social psychologists that each child is "social" by nature, it has become clear that we are social beings connected by a social network. That network is what creates our brains, and the coherence of our brains. It is the source of our interior lives. Our interior lives are not self-generated, but generated in relationship, and are a function of those relationships, so that if we do not have some sense of safety in our interpersonal relationships it's very difficult to have internal safety. We are often told that we can, in fact, not be influenced by other people, and not let other people influence us. We doubt that's the case.

We talk about dissociation as one of the cornerstones of some pathologies. There are times when, because we are so anxious because of a painful event, we can dissociate and therefore not feel our context. That's a defense against feeling the context, which would allow us to have another emotion. There is a one-to-one correlation between the quality of the interpersonal and the quality of our inner world—what we call subjectivity.

Consider someone who's been single for a long time and doesn't want to be—they long for a partner. Perhaps they've said, "You know I have a lot of self-judgment. I'm not sure that I can really love someone in the way that I feel this potential in my heart. I don't know if I can receive their love either." We would help them begin to look at those thoughts in terms of their origins. On the one hand—how old are the patterns? Usually if they're chronic, they're old. The second thing that people don't often do after they do the excavation is ask: What is the function of those thoughts? What is this protecting you from? What kinds of experiments are you willing to do?

When our son was twenty-one years old, he told us he had a lot of social anxiety. He was going to a therapist, but spoke to us about it as well. What he was doing to remedy it was put himself into environments that he was afraid of, just for a little bit at a time, and then when he felt anxious, backing out, processing the experience, and then going back in and taking it a little further. In addition, he was putting himself in different kinds of uncomfortable social situations and processing those. What he was doing was getting some reality data that could help him understand that the possibilities he imagined as catastrophic might not be that catastrophic. This was essentially cognitive therapy—behavioral therapy—but you have to experiment. You have to put yourself in the context and do that.

Another thing we have discovered is the power of ambivalence when people get into relational conversations about what they would like or what they fear—especially couples who are not sure if they want to stay in the relationship. If we're ambivalent, it seems that our brain doesn't know what to do. It goes into a free flow and cycle. When the brain is not engaged in some sort of intentional project, either being creative or protective, we become anxious, and so that ambivalence feeds on itself.

Take, for example, people who are in cohabitating relationships who are ambivalent about getting married but are there to experiment with how to be married. When they decide that they are going to commit and get married, when they move from ambivalence to commitment, a great deal of anxiety occurs. The brain now knows it has to do something. It has to go to work, but sitting in the ambivalence had not allowed for much growth. So, the ambivalence about what it is that they now want tends to interfere with progress toward any goal they might have.

If a couple or individual is stuck in this place of ambivalence, and they really want to grow, really want to move toward some decision, to get an outcome, they need to become intentional. That is, make a decision, commit to it, and engage it. They begin to collect and sort the data. We ask people to look at their ambivalence, because the ambivalence protects them from some fearful imagined outcome.

In our book *Receiving Love*, we emphasized the importance and challenge of letting love in. That book came out of a clinical situation with a couple. A woman was complaining about, what was for her, a very important issue—she wanted her husband to thank her for cooking dinner. For her husband, this was trivial, and for many people it might be the same. The husband was opposed to this because he worked every day to make the money to buy the house and the food for dinner, and he wasn't asking for thanks for all he was doing. "She should just do what she is supposed to do," he said. "That's what we do. That's your role. This is my role."

Still, this was *really* important to her. We did a brief exploration back to her childhood, and she saw that when she was a child she was basically invisible to her mother. Nothing she did was ever okay with her mother—she could never please her. This was very damaging and left her in a disempowered mode. We talked about that for a while, then pushed her a little further toward what would happen if she actually let herself feel good about what she was doing. She shared a fantasy that her mother would really reject her.

When she told her husband about it, he understood this and became empathic, saying, "I didn't know that was going to be so important and *is* so important to you. I care about you. I love you and I want to say how much I appreciate you for cooking our meals. I know it's important, and I'm going to thank you for every dinner from now on."

The woman's response was interesting. She got angry! She said, "You're just doing that because we are in therapy, but you don't really mean it." That shocked me because she had done her work and he had done his work. I asked her to go deeper, and she reached a fantasy, a memory, that was a catastrophic outcome expectation: if she accepted love, her mother would reject her. Her mother had said to her, "You will never be loved, you're not worth being loved, and anytime a man tells you that he loves you in the future, don't believe it." What she found was that if she accepted her husband's love, she would violate the internal injunction built into her mind from this transaction with her mother when she was young. Receiving love was more dangerous for her than living without love and complaining about it.

This situation made sense, for the first time, of hundreds of couples who had difficulty when they began to make progress. Originally, we had interpreted this phenomenon as the chaos of moving out of a stasis into some new flow of energy, which produces normal anxiety. And it *does*, but in this particular case, when it's intransigent it's usually rooted in some unconscious catastrophic outcome—if you let love in, something terrible will happen—so that receiving love is more dangerous than giving love or doing without love.

We can apply this understanding to compliments. Many people aren't good at accepting them. We might say, "Hey, that was a good speech," and they'd reply, "I really wasn't on today and didn't think the speech was that good." We might say, "You look beautiful in that dress," and they'd reply, "No I don't. This old rag makes me look fat."

Helen and I interviewed hundreds of people and asked them to talk about the experience of their rejection of the compliment. Their replies were interesting and a pattern emerged. Some said that if they let in the compliment that they did well, it would establish expectations that they always function at a high level. Others assumed that people were always insincere, so they didn't believe the compliments. Most people told us that if they let love in, it required them to release the architecture of their self-concept, in which they were people who had been negatively valued in the past. To let that stasis be uncovered and impacted by a compliment would produce more anxiety than living with the equilibrium they had.

How do you release the defense and teach people that allowing love in won't result in catastrophe? The first step is to understand where the defense comes from and the catastrophic outcome of allowing oneself to move beyond the defense. The second is to collect data over time until it is undeniable.

The general message was that if we *really* let in compliments, if we really accept love from people, it will change our self-configuration. Many of us have configured ourselves around some "smaller person," but we can open up to being a bigger, different person. The results are positive, but the process can be anxiety producing because possibility is inherently unpredictable. Think about it—when we're comfortable in our self-configuration or idea of ourselves that has served us for so long, we can pretty much predict most situations. As neuroscience teaches us, our brain really likes to know what is coming next.

Someone who is able to fully let in love is someone who is willing to live in the mystery of who they are. They have to become comfortable with this unpredictability and release the architecture of the self they have lived in and carried around for so long. It is a concept; it's not us. When we release that, we go into "not knowing" who we are, and that's anxiety provoking because we don't have the ability to know who we are, much less how others will respond to us.

Moving into the mystery of "not knowing" is essential to the experience of coming to know who we really are—magnificent creatures, connected to an amazing tapestry of being. When we are aware of this and have a felt sense of connection, we can live in joy. Helen and I have become convinced that when we are not living in joy it's because something has triggered our anxiety. Then we go into our defenses and experience ourselves as separate. If we are separate, then we have to be self-protective. Yet, when we experience ourselves as *being with*, being one with, belonging to, or being a part of something, we experience *connecting*—not being connected, but connecting itself. If we are not feeling that, it is because something has ruptured the felt sense of connecting and we have insulated ourselves with some sort of defense mechanism.

This applies to self-judgment or self-criticism as much as it does to relationship. Helen and I, as partners in life and work, and as co-creators of Imago, have been in this conversation about authentic connecting for thirty-five years. One of the things we have evolved while dealing with negativity, individually and in our relationship, is the concept of curiosity about the mystery of self. What we teach couples is that, instead of reacting to negativity with negativity or trying to correct it and heal it with positive input, become curious and ask what's going on when your partner triggers something in you. What works in relationship also works with each of us as individuals. When we can go into that curiosity, it regulates anxiety and we feel better about ourselves.

According to neuroscientists, the brain's default is always negative because the brain was shaped over millions of years to *not* assume if you heard a snap in the forest that it was somebody coming to play with us or to have sex with us. Repetitive experience of being someone else's lunch, rather than having a playmate, changed the anticipation from pleasure to danger, building the negative as the default of the brain. The negative default of the brain will always be self-protective. We are always going to take the self-protective position. In our workshops and seminars, Helen has become accustomed to saying: "You can't control your first thought, but you can certainly control your second thought." One of the best ways to control it is to get some data. Curiosity can negate the fantasy and elicit new data that leads to a sense of safety. When that happens, we experience the joy of connecting, which is the felt sense of being. And that is all we need, or want. It is that for which all other yearnings are a precursor.

embodying
SELF-ACCEPTANCE

8

COMPASSION FOR THE SELF-CRITIC

Kristin Neff

We know how to be kind and compassionate to others
when they're feeling bad about themselves or are
suffering in some way. We know what to say and do.
We just have to remember to do it for ourselves.

In our culture, people are becoming increasingly aware of the need for more compassion in their lives, not only for others, but also for themselves. This is the result of some societal shifts. A big one stems from the self-esteem movement of the 1970s and 1980s, which delivered, but not in the way we had hoped. This movement came from very good intentions. A lot of humanistic psychologists and other psychologists recognized the problem of self-hate and the lack of self-acceptance, and how much suffering that caused. There was a shift toward trying to help people feel good about themselves, and many of us thought that was about raising their self-esteem—a positive judgment or evaluation of oneself. This filtered into the schools and into therapy, and much of it was very good and very useful.

The problem is that it wasn't very refined. People didn't pay enough attention to *how* people raised their self-esteem, and so things backfired. Children were raised to think, "I'm special and above average. I'm important. If I'm not special and above average, it's not okay; there is something wrong with me." People became very self-focused and felt entitled because, as they were growing up, they were told that they *should* be entitled to special treatment. In fact, one of the unintended consequences of the self-esteem movement is what has been called the "narcissism epidemic" or the "Me Generation." Now we're realizing the false promises that the self-esteem movement gave us, and we're trying to understand how we can relate to ourselves positively in a healthy way. That's the shift—from judging ourselves positively to relating to ourselves kindly. It seems that self-compassion is a very good answer.

One of the key ways to relate to ourselves positively is by letting go of our view of self-criticism as the problem. This belief causes a lot of suffering. What we've found in our teaching of self-compassion is that we need to have a lot of compassion for our inner critic. That nagging voice that says, "You're not good enough. You need to do more of this; you need to do more of that"—although painful—actually has good intentions. It comes from a desire to maintain social relationships, to keep ourselves from being rejected, to keep ourselves safe. It originates from a place of care, but it's been twisted—we think that if we criticize ourselves, we'll be in control and able to force ourselves to be the person we want to be so that we will be accepted, loved, and safe.

I teach self-compassion workshops, and for years, I tried to help people motivate themselves with compassion instead of self-criticism. I had created many exercises, but nothing was quite working until I introduced the importance of having compassion for the self-critic. We have to understand that it is trying to protect and motivate us (often in the voice of a two-year-old child having a tantrum), even if it's counterproductive.

Typically, we judge the *self-judge*. "Oh, there she goes again," that "inner bitch," or whatever we want to call her. This judgment just adds more fuel to the fire. To be compassionate means to ask: Why is that critical voice there? How is it actually trying to help me? Can I understand where it comes from beyond my early childhood experience? *How is it trying to keep me safe?*

If we look at self-criticism physiologically, it taps into the threat defense system: it triggers the amygdala; it releases cortisol; and it gears us up for the fight-or-flight response. This system evolved to deal with physical threats, like a lion chasing us, but the threat nowadays is to our self-concept. So, when we see a flaw in ourselves, or we fail in some way, we feel endangered and that there is a big problem. There is a problem, but the problem is *us*. When we attack the problem, we attack ourselves. We release cortisol and adrenaline—causing us a lot of stress—all in an unconscious attempt to keep ourselves safe.

Both self-criticism and self-compassion are systems designed to help us feel safe. The problem with self-criticism is we're tapping into a system that is effective when we are running away from lions but terrible when we gain five pounds or disappoint our mother because it makes us depressed—it makes things worse.

What self-compassion does is move our sense of safety from the reptilian threat defense system to the mammalian caregiving system—the other system designed to help keep us safe. Mammals are born very immature, so in order for a mammal to feel safe when they're young, they respond to close connection, soft touch, and especially physical warmth from the mother. That releases things like oxytocin and opiates that lower cortisol, activate the parasympathetic nervous system, and deactivate the sympathetic nervous system, calming us down.

The reason I like to talk about physiology is that one of the quickest and easiest ways to switch from self-criticism to self-compassion is with a physical gesture of affection. In our workshops, we teach people to put their hands on their hearts, because we mammals are designed to respond to warm, soothing touch, to gentle pressure with the intent to soothe. Then we feel safe. We need to learn to connect our feeling of safety to this feeling of compassion, of care, and "I love you just the way you are." Maybe we need to make some changes—not because we are inadequate, but because we love ourselves and don't want to suffer. Once we do that, everything shifts.

But people are often not self-compassionate because they really believe they need their self-criticism to motivate themselves. In parenting, we used to have the idea of "Spare the rod, spoil the child." We used to think that children needed harsh discipline, and we really thought that we had to use critical methods with children to get them to work hard and try hard. Our parenting styles have changed, and we now know that harsh criticism or corporal punishment makes children depressed and actually isn't effective at all. However, for some strange reason, even people who are wonderful, sensitive parents with their children still use harsh punishment with themselves, because they think they need their self-criticism to motivate themselves. They don't realize that self-criticism makes us anxious, stressed, afraid of failure, and puts us in the worst possible mindset to do our best. Our culture supports self-criticism as a way to motivate ourselves.

We can learn to motivate ourselves with compassion. If we go back to the parenting example, think about how a parent would best motivate their child to reach their goals. Let's say there is a mother, and her teenage daughter has a failing grade in math. This is a problem because the girl wants to go on to college; she has goals and aspirations. There are two ways to motivate that child. The first would be through criticism. The mother could say to the child when she comes home with her failing grade, "I'm so ashamed of you. You disgust me. You're a failure. You'll never amount to anything. Go to your room." Those words make you cringe, don't they? But isn't that exactly what we often say to ourselves? Do you think it's going to motivate the daughter? It might for a short time—she might do her homework because she's afraid of her mother's criticism, but she's going to lose faith in herself, she might drop math, and it's going to put her in a terrible mind state the next time she takes a test, worrying, "Oh my god, what if I fail again?"

What if the mother takes a compassionate approach, and first says, "Oh, I'm sorry you've failed. You must be feeling bad about yourself. It's okay. I love you anyway. It happens to all of us. It happened to me when I was your age. But I know you want to go to college. I know how important it is to you. I know you need to get your math grades up to do so. How can I support you? Let me know how to help you reach your goals."

An encouraging, supportive approach with the message that "I believe in you and I know you can do it," is going to be so much more effective with a child. It's the same with ourselves. We can use encouragement and support to meet our goals. And the thing about self-compassion is, it is concerned with the alleviation of suffering, and if we are not reaching a goal that is important to us, a goal that may be possible for us, whatever the goal happens to be, we are going to suffer. So if we love ourselves and we care about ourselves, we are going to want to do everything we can to reach our full potential, just like a mother wants her daughter to reach her full potential. That's how compassion, support, love, and kindness become a resource for motivation. We just need to catch ourselves when we're trying to motivate ourselves with harsh self-judgment, and adopt this new habit.

That's why the mindfulness piece, the awareness piece, is so important. The absolute starting point has to be noticing when self-criticism is happening. Mindfulness can help us develop a refined ear for the self-critical voice. Even when it is very subtle, we can still hear, "Oh, my tone when I talked to myself was kind of harsh." We need to learn to notice the self-critical voice and the suffering associated with it, practice building a new response, and then receive the positive reinforcement of the good effect it has on us.

Awareness and practice are the way to change habits, including compassion for what's driving the habit. The more I get into this, the more I am realizing how important it is to have compassion for what is driving the habit. Because, otherwise, if the self-critic doesn't feel heard and validated—honored, really—for the work it's doing, it's going to keep trying to shout out to you, "Hey. Hey, listen to me. Listen to me." By saying to the self-critic, "Thank you for trying to help me. I think I may try another way of moving forward, try to motivate myself with some kindness this time, but I appreciate what you're trying to do for me. Thanks for your efforts." Then the self-critic says, "Well, I feel heard. I can maybe chill out a little now." There actually is a therapy method called Internal Family Systems that bases its whole approach on understanding the function of all the conflicting parts of ourselves and giving them compassion. I've found it remarkably effective for myself, and with other people, in changing habits. You give that voice what it needs—and what it needs is to be heard—and then it doesn't have to assert itself so strongly.

When we criticize ourselves, we reinforce the illusion of control—that we should have been able to do it perfectly. It's almost scarier to acknowledge the reality that we aren't perfect, aren't in control, and we can't always do it right than it is to acknowledge the pain of our own vulnerability. It's quite scary to admit that we are limited human beings with very little control. If we are willing to accept how not in control we are, we would have to totally re-examine what the "self" is. Who is in charge? What is this "self" that I think is in control of my life? We must examine the whole question of identity. I'm a practicing Buddhist, so I've seen this in my personal practice. How, when I start questioning this sense of the separate self who's in control—who is able to make the decisions and have the results I want—it does start falling apart. It's a little scary, at first.

It's another reason why we need self-compassion. If we are going to let go of self-criticism, including the sense of safety it provides us (even though it is an illusionary safety, it still provides you some sense of safety), we need to replace it with something. We need to be able to catch ourselves and say, "Okay, maybe I'm not a separate self who's in control, but I'm a part of an interconnected whole, and I love myself, and I care about myself. That's why it's okay." More than that, we need to say, "I'm here to support myself in those difficult times."

Difficult things happen—you lose your job, or you get cancer, or something else you have no control over—but you do have *access* to an amazing resource—the ability to be a supportive, encouraging friend to yourself. Once you start to trust that, and trust that you can give *you* what *you* need in difficult times, then you start to build a new and more reliable sense of safety.

One important way to soften our inner criticism and have compassion for our imperfection is by recognizing our common humanity—everyone feels inadequate, flawed, and imperfect. It is part of the human experience to fail, to blow it sometimes; you are not alone in this. When we make mistakes, however, we tend to feel that something has gone wrong—that the baseline should be "everything is going swimmingly." When it's not, we feel that we're somehow abnormal, that it's only me that is going through this right now. That feeling of loss of connection is incredibly frightening, because evolutionarily, if we were rejected from the group, we were at the mercy of the lions. So an important way you can soften your self-criticism and create a kinder approach to yourself is by remembering common humanity. When we do this, every moment of feeling inadequate actually becomes an opportunity for connection.

If you practice self-compassion in your life, you'll see it's really just a series of on-the-spot interventions. We can start with the tiny little moments throughout the day. "Oh, I spilled the milk!" Catch yourself before you judge yourself and say, "What a klutz." Just remember, "Wait a minute; I spilled the milk. It's okay." "Everyone spills milk sometimes." "It's just spilled milk." "Don't cry over . . . " It has to be in-the-moment practice in order to be effective, and integrated into actual life so that it's a habit in place ready to help handle the big stuff. If you are just self-compassionate on the meditation cushion and not in your daily life, it's not going to be that effective.

If you find yourself feeling bad about yourself or judging yourself, try making a physical gesture of self-compassion. Then, using a kind tone of voice, say words that convey care and concern, like, "I'm so sorry it's really hard right now," or "I'm here for you and you can rely on me," or "I love you anyway." Say things to yourself you would say to a child who was distressed or to a good friend who is suffering. In fact, a study by Leah B. Shapira and Myriam Mongrain showed that speaking to oneself as a good friend for seven days straight lowers depression for three months and raises happiness for six months. It's amazing. By doing this we make everything more workable. It's actually easier than we think. We know how to be kind and compassionate to others when they're feeling bad about themselves or are suffering in some way. We know what to say and do. We just have to remember to do it for ourselves.

Like Pema Chödrön said, "Start where you are." The idea is that even if we are lost in the throes of self-criticism or are feeling intense shame, we can have compassion for how hard it is to feel that shame. Maybe it's too much to dive directly into the root cause of the shame. Or maybe it's too overwhelming. At least we can say, "Wow, it's really hard to be feeling so full of shame right now."

For me, self-compassion is a personal journey. Everyone needs self-compassion, but I joke that there is a reason that self-compassion is my life's work—I need a lot of it. I write about this in my book *Self-Compassion*. I actually got into learning about self-compassion through Buddhist meditation when I had just gone through a very messy divorce. I was feeling a lot of shame, a lot of social judgment. It was also the year I was finishing up my PhD at Berkeley, so there was all the stress of finishing, getting a job, and so on. I thought I would learn to meditate. On the very first night, the woman leading the meditation group spoke about having compassion for ourselves, as well as for others. It was as if a light bulb went off in my head. *"Wow! This is what I need right now—I need some support. I need to stop judging myself. I need to start practicing being kind."* It made a huge difference in how I handled what I was going through at the time.

Self-compassion came into play for me in an even bigger way when my son was diagnosed with autism. Luckily, I already had a steady self-compassion practice—at the time he was diagnosed, I had been practicing between five to seven years. I knew when I received the diagnosis that in addition to finding out about treatment options for my son, I had to put a great deal of attention on helping myself get through the natural reactions of grief—the sadness, fear, not knowing what to do. I really took the time to be there for myself and give myself compassion.

I saw how the more compassionate I was with myself, the more I was able to give of myself, the more I could give him—and the more I gave, the more I helped him. It has made such a huge difference. When you open your heart, you open your heart. Sometimes you need to open it to yourself before you can really open it to others.

The Self-Compassion Break

There are three main components to self-compassion, at least as I've defined it. One is self-kindness versus harsh self-judgment. The second is this sense of common humanity versus isolation—framing our experience in light of the imperfect shared human experience. Then, there is being mindful of our suffering, as opposed to ignoring it or maybe running with the dramatic story line of how horrible things are. We teach something called the "self-compassion break" for these moments of self-criticism, when we are feeling inadequate, that evokes these three components. It goes like this:

- Think of something in your life that's causing you a lot of suffering, something you are struggling with, maybe something you are judging yourself for, or something in daily life that comes up naturally.

- Then, say the following phrase to yourself: *"This is the moment of suffering."* You might use other words like, *"This is really hard right now."* This is a reminder to be mindful of the pain we're in.

- The next phrase is: *"Suffering is part of life."* Again, use words that feel natural to you. Maybe something like, *"It's so human to feel this way,"* or *"I'm not alone in this."* This is a reminder of our common humanity.

- Then, adopt a self-compassionate posture—it could be putting your hands on your heart or something else that feels soothing and comforting. Then feeling the warm response of your hands, say, *"May I be kind to myself in this moment. May I give myself the compassion I need."*

- Finally, say any other words that come to reinforce that message. A very useful tool is to think about what you'd say to a close friend going through the exact same thing you are, then say the same thing to yourself.

You can do this in a slow way, almost like a mini-meditation, or you can do it very quickly. Sometimes these memorized phrases arise spontaneously, like a mantra: *This is the moment of suffering. Suffering is part of life. May I be kind to myself in this moment. May I give myself the compassion I need.* When combined with a physical gesture, this can be incredibly powerful.

9

STAYING LOYAL TO ONE'S SELF: INHABITING THE BODY

Judith Blackstone

We can really experience this ground of oneness.
It is the basis of our deepest acceptance of others and ourselves.

When we inhabit our body, we shift from knowing ourselves as an idea, such as "I am a teacher," to having an actual, quality-rich experience of who we are. We create a deep intimacy with ourselves—this is the basis of self-acceptance. Self-acceptance—both psychological and spiritual—is an extremely important topic. Although there is plenty of psychological attention paid to it, I don't think there's enough focus on it in our teachings and conversations about spirituality.

In the more advanced phases of both spiritual and psychological maturity, psychological healing and spiritual realization are the same process. In my understanding, spiritual awakening is uncovering the subtlest dimension of ourselves, a dimension that we experience as subtle consciousness, pervading our body and our environment as a unity. Because this spiritual dimension pervades our bodies at the same time as it pervades our environment, we can only uncover it if we are able to inhabit our bodies. Inhabiting our body depends on a certain degree of psychological healing and self-acceptance. We need to be able to make deep contact with ourselves in order to open to unified, pervasive consciousness. In this way, psychological health—that quality-rich experience of ourselves as individuals—is a necessary component of spiritual openness.

This is why we can say that self-acceptance is a spiritual practice. It is necessary for spiritual awakening. The reason that we need to practice it, to cultivate it, is that most of us grow up with some amount of self-doubt or shame about ourselves, and even self-loathing. Because human beings are not perfect, we do not love perfectly. However, whenever we were not loved as young children, whenever we were rejected, we tended to reject ourselves. We all grow up, to some extent, overly critical of ourselves, anticipating failure or poor behavior, watching ourselves from the outside to guard against making mistakes. This self-rejection and this objectifying of ourselves prevents us from the kind of deep contact with ourselves that is necessary for spiritual openness.

I will explain what I mean by the "quality-rich" experience of ourselves that occurs when we inhabit our body, and how these qualities help us develop self-acceptance. The interior space of the body is not blank space. Each part of the body has a particular quality. When we inhabit that part of our body, when we live in that part of ourselves, we experience that quality. For example, when we live inside our brain, we experience the quality of intelligence. We can feel our intelligence as it emerges when we make deep contact with the internal space inside our heads. When we inhabit our chest, we experience the quality of love. We do not need to love someone or something in order to feel this love; it is always there. We just need to dwell there, to be present within the internal space of our chest. When we inhabit our throat, we can experience the quality of our voice, our potential to speak. When we inhabit our mid-section, between our ribs and pelvis, we experience an actual feeling of power. This is pure power like a waterfall—not over someone, but power that is both enlivening and supportive. When we inhabit our pelvis, we experience the quality of our sexuality.

These qualities are innate; we do not have to imagine them. They emerge spontaneously when we inhabit our body. They are also universal. Although they may be slightly different in each of us, they are similar enough for us to recognize them in other people. For example, most of us can recognize when someone is feeling love, or has love in his or her voice or eyes. Although these qualities are hard to put into words, we know when we are experiencing them. These are ways we can really *feel* ourselves existing; they are the qualities of our own aliveness.

Experiencing these qualities within our body is an important part of the deep intimacy with ourselves that is the basis of self-acceptance. It is difficult to dislike ourselves when we actually feel love in our chest as an inherent quality. It is difficult to feel stupid, or to have to guard against saying or doing something stupid, when we experience the quality of our intelligence within our brain. It is difficult to feel afraid of other people when we experience the quality of power within our mid-section.

Inhabiting the body is different from being aware of your body. Here is a brief exercise to help you experience this difference:

- Start by becoming aware of your hands. As you become aware of your hands, you may feel their temperature, whether they are hot or cold. You may feel that your hands are relaxed or tense. That is becoming aware of your hands.

- Now enter into your hands. Experience yourself living within your hands. See if you can feel that you are the internal space of your hands—that it is part of who you are.

- You may be able to feel this same "living within" in other parts of your body: your feet and legs, your whole torso, your arms and hands, your neck, your head. Then see if you can inhabit your body as a whole, so that you feel that you *are* the internal space of your body. If we say that the body is the temple, you are sitting inside the temple, with nothing left out. Even with your eyes open, you have your own "temple" to sit inside, your own internal space.

In the Realization Process, the method I teach for embodied nondual awakening, this "living within the body," is the basis of attuning to ourselves as the pervasive space of subtle, unified consciousness, pervading the whole internal space of our body and our environment at the same time. We also attune to the innate qualities within the body and experience how these qualities resonate and are part of our oneness with other people.

By inhabiting the body, we can remain connected with ourselves—to the desires, needs, and responses that occur within our own body—while feeling open to, and even experiencing oneness, with other people. Even if they are critical of us or reject us, we do not reject ourselves. We are still there within our own body. We can remain loyal to ourselves even during painful and abrasive encounters with others.

This loyalty to ourselves can help us accept our imperfections. Take body image, for example, since many of us are ashamed of something about our body. Knowing that there is intelligence, love, and power within our bodies can help us love and accept our bodies as the vessels of these innate qualities. When we have this deep, rich, internal knowledge of ourselves, how others view us becomes much less important. Then we can lower our guard. We become less self-conscious and more spontaneous, and we can let other people really see us. Accepting our imperfections means not having to hide from other people. We do not have to adjust ourselves to appear a little bit better in their eyes.

There's a reciprocal effect when we accept our own limitations—we accept others in the same way. When we allow people to really see us, we are also able to see them. We begin to recognize that the people around us are not perfect either—this is the human condition. The basis of our humanness is something that we all share, and it is quite wonderful: it is made of love and intelligence, and all of the innate qualities that are a natural part of our being.

I think that the process of psychotherapy is important to spiritual awakening because it helps us really see how little we do accept ourselves. In my work as a psychotherapist and spiritual teacher, I help people to accept their own narrative, how they formed themselves as children. We often don't know what our negative beliefs are and how many we have until we actually experience them being heard and received by another relatively nonjudgmental human being. In addition, when people become aware of their own psychological narrative, they may begin to feel true compassion for how they managed to survive the various challenges of their childhood environment.

Inhabiting the body may be a scary and uncomfortable process at first. As children, we constricted our bodies in order to protect ourselves against painful or overwhelming circumstances. In order to inhabit our body, we need to release some of these protective constrictions, along with the painful memories and emotions that are bound up with them. As we come back into our bodies, the first thing we often encounter is pain. For some people, it may even feel dangerous. If being conspicuous as children meant that we became the target of a parent's rage, for example, it may feel that we will be in danger again if we become present within our body. Inhabiting ourselves, all the way through the interior volume of ourselves, is actually the safest place that we can be. That subtle unified consciousness that we uncover, that pervades our body and environment as a whole, cannot be broken. It feels like who we really are, and yet it is just consciousness, just transparency. In Zen Buddhism, they describe this unified spiritual ground of our being as "I have never moved from the beginning." Once we know ourselves as this spiritual dimension of consciousness, we cannot be psychologically injured by another person. We still feel deeply—and we may feel hurt, afraid, or angry—but our emotions move through the unbreakable ground of our being without diminishing or shattering us. We become resilient.

In my book *Belonging Here*, I describe how spiritually sensitive people may have particular challenges as children that need to be addressed and healed in order for them to become spiritually awakened. By spiritually sensitive, I mean that they may be particularly attuned to the sensory stimuli in the environment, or to the emotional vibrations of the people around them. They may have a kind of emotional or mental depth that causes them, as children, to become the caretakers of the adults in their lives. Because of their sensitivity, they constrict, fragment, or unground themselves more severely than, for example, their siblings or their peers. They may have a particular challenge with self-acceptance because of their acute attunement to peoples' reactions. As a result, they may grow up to be extremely self-conscious, and to feel deep shame in response to even mild criticism. The good news is that their sensitivity can also make it easier for them to have inward contact with themselves. For example, just as they can easily attune to their environment, they can attune inward and uncover the spiritual dimension of themselves. If they have spent their lives loving and caring for other people, they can find the source of that love within their body and practice directing that love toward themselves as well.

When we inhabit the body, we uncover a natural internal unity at the same time as we uncover the unity of our individual body and our environment. We realize ourselves as the one ground of subtle consciousness that pervades our body and environment as a whole. This means that we experience our wholeness as individuals at the same time as we transcend our individuality.

In the body, this pervasive space is experienced both as emptiness—as if we were an empty vessel—and at the same time, it is experienced as presence, endowed with the qualities that I have described. This ground of emptiness and quality-rich presence is accessible to all of us, and it is the same in all of us. That is what is so amazing. We can really experience this ground of oneness. It is the basis of our deepest acceptance of others and ourselves.

10

NOT SELF-ACCEPTANCE, BUT AN ACCEPTING SELF

Bruce Tift

Successful self-acceptance is akin to an autoimmune disease that's in remission, waiting to become a problem again when we have to deal with some stress or life crisis.

Who among us has not had the experience of attacking ourselves? For some, it happens off and on and is a disturbance we can work with. For others, it's almost a way of life, with a very painful, almost continual, sense of torturing ourselves. As a therapist, it is rare that this experience is not part of what I address in the work of reducing unnecessary suffering. In this work, though, I think it's important to discriminate between an aggressive response to what we may be experiencing and the idea of being aggressive to one's "self."

I've found that it's very workable to gradually cultivate an attitude of unconditional kindness toward whatever we may be experiencing. The basis of this practice is taking experiential ownership of everything that arises in our awareness. However, it's actually impossible to accept a "self" that's different than the "I" that's accepting it. The project of self-acceptance is really a project of the divided self, which is a hallucination. I have to imagine that parts of my experiencing are "not-me," while other parts are "me." On the biological level, our immune systems are designed to attack anything that is non-self. Maintaining our belief in being divided against ourselves can be understood as analogous to an autoimmune disease. Even if we can accept this "self," it's still alien to "I" and a potential threat. Successful self-acceptance is like an autoimmune disease that's in remission, waiting to become a problem again when we have to deal with some stress or life crisis.

This sense of being divided against oneself is very pervasive and compelling as a drama in which our worth as a person seems to be hanging in the balance. Unfortunately, it generates a lot of unnecessary suffering and confusion. Fortunately, it has no basis in reality and can gradually be dissolved. From a Western view, this assumption of being divided and problematic is probably an unavoidable developmental stage to be experienced and worked through. As young children, we all have to disconnect from or disown aspects of ourselves to fit in with our parents, our world, our gender training, and so on. It's intelligent, healthy, creative, and necessary. If every time I yell at my parents, they hit me or withhold love, it's smart to learn to disconnect from my angry feelings. If it's unacceptable to disappoint my parents, I may organize my life around achievement and success, avoiding at all cost the panic of feeling like a failure. Growing up in complex emotional environments, almost all of us have to sacrifice parts of ourselves for our emotional survival and to get the most love possible.

This capacity to apparently disown aspects of ourselves, to push problematic feelings out of awareness, serves us and tends to become internalized as character structure persisting into adulthood. The very real benefit we get comes with a price tag. This young survival strategy leaves us feeling divided against ourselves: now there's a part of us that's dangerous, shameful, unacceptable, or overwhelming. I find that it's usually not until someone is in his or her thirties or forties that these young ways of self-care begin to exhaust themselves. We receive more and more evidence that they are no longer supported by the truth of our experience and are no longer necessary.

Challenging the very strategies that have helped us survive and function well in the world is anxiety provoking, and so most of us have contradictory feelings about doing this work. This is the basic theme of Western depth psychology. We must deal with the back and forth between wanting to live with more sense of aliveness and wholeness, which requires that we give up our young survival strategies, and at the same time wanting to still feel safe and keep our familiar sense of self, which means hanging on to these strategies. A common, though unconscious, response to this dilemma is to invest in the project of self-acceptance. We can work on accepting disowned feelings, such as anger or failure, without ever addressing the fundamental young strategy of feeling like divided and problematic selves. Only now, our "problem" is lack of self-acceptance. As long as we have "not accepted ourselves," we can remain in the safety of withholding our full presence and vulnerability while claiming that we're committed to feeling whole.

The unconscious function of our self-acceptance project is to feel like we're working on our fundamental sense of not trusting ourselves, with no danger of actually resolving this drama. We claim to ourselves that we'll show up when we feel safe and whole, but of course, continuing our fantasy of feeling divided against ourselves insures that we never feel safe and whole. When we were children, it was smart to not show all of who we were, and we did this by not being aware of our full range of experience. Now that we are adults, it may be smart to own all of who we are and to know that we have a choice about what we show to others.

Western therapy tends to be issue-specific. We address re-enactment patterns in our relationships, bring our self-image up to date, learn more skillful ways to communicate and have conflict, and so on. As we learn to cultivate a more positive sense of self, it becomes easier to accept that self. And because in Western culture we take the "self" to be a self-evident, existing reality, much of therapy is about improving and accepting this self.

From a Buddhist view, we take a more generic approach. We practice an attitude of unconditional acceptance of all of our experiencing, rather than developing a self that's worthy of acceptance. Unconditional means everything, without exception. Even our feelings of being divided are accepted with no effort to heal or resolve them. When we relate to all experience as being equally valid, whether we like it or not, we address the heart of the issue. We are engaging with every moment of experiencing with awareness, embodiment, and kindness, and it becomes increasingly difficult to sustain our dramas of disowning disturbing aspects of who we are.

Awareness is central to a Buddhist approach. It refers to what is most basic, always present in our experiencing: a nonconceptual knowing, an open engagement without bias or preference, experienced as inherent freedom. It's very difficult to intervene in any habitual patterns if we're not aware of them. Holding our experience in awareness allows a type of open inquiry with no predetermined outcome.

The practice of embodiment means that we are willing to continually return our attention to immediate sensation-level experience with no interpretation at all. We discover what is most true in this present moment, rather than going with our historically conditioned interpretations, which are about what used to be true.

Kindness is a heart-based relating to everything that arises with a "yes," a warm engagement. It's the opposite of our usual aggression toward aspects of our experience that we don't like. Applying these practices in daily life can gradually dissolve our painful project of self-acceptance.

To use a classic Buddhist analogy, if we walk out of our home onto the lawn and step on a snake, we'll jump away and run into the house, thankful that we are safe. However, if we're willing to go back outside and examine what frightened us, we may find it was a garden hose. If we don't investigate, we'll assume that our response was accurate and necessary and perhaps even begin to avoid going outside. Let's say that snake is a feeling of shame, triggered by some life circumstance, but actually a lifelong vulnerability with origins in our childhood. Perhaps we hurt someone's feelings, fail at something, or act selfishly. We may try to escape from the painful and familiar feeling of shame by attacking ourselves, compromising our integrity to purchase approval, avoiding conflict, getting angry or intellectual, and so on.

All of these responses tend to unconsciously confirm that our feeling of shame really is a problem, a threat to our survival. Our very avoidance of a feeling confirms that it is unworkable, that we are unworkable. However, if we're willing to go back into our feeling of shame and investigate it with the practices of awareness, embodiment, and kindness, we may find no harm or damage, no evidence about our worth as a person. There's disturbance: we might feel nauseated, our heart may pound or our throat might constrict, we may feel numb. But we won't find shame as an immediate embodied sensation. We'll only find shame in our interpretations about this vulnerability, just as we won't find guilt, or abandonment, or jealousy, or failure, or any of our favorite problems. We discover that our immediate experience is workable because our state of mind is workable. Our state of mind is workable because we will engage with anything and exclude nothing, finding disturbance but no problem. The snake is just a garden hose. The feelings that prove we are not acceptable are just intense sensations in our bodies toward which we can learn to direct kindness.

This work is difficult. It requires discipline to take ourselves into our familiar fears. It goes against both our personal history and our evolutionary biology that says: if you feel unsafe, head for the hills or fight the threat. It's counter-instinctual. Actually, sanity can be understood as a counter-instinctual practice. It's always easier to avoid fear and disturbance than to go into these scary experiences. Avoiding the feelings now, as adults, that were, in fact, unworkable as children, perpetuates our investment in pretending to be divided against ourselves. Participating in exactly what we don't want to feel, as embodied sensation, without interpretation, with kindness, is what dissolves the fantasy of our being problematic persons.

As we practice with this understanding, with these disciplines, we may find ourselves progressing through an unfolding series of stages or experiences, with each stage an expression of our increasing willingness and capacity to bring unconditional presence and kindness into our familiar conditioned experiencing. It seems necessary to begin with an *awareness* of just how pervasively and powerfully our habits of self-aggression are continually arising. This can feel discouraging at first, but it's already an act of kindness to look more directly at the truth of our experiencing. We can then gradually learn to *tolerate* these familiar patterns. The practice of embodied immediacy helps us recognize that we are not harmed by staying in relation to what we don't want to feel.

Remaining embodied with our disturbance cultivates an experience of *acceptance*. We wish we didn't have to feel our shame, or fear, or rage, but these familiar feelings don't seem to be going away, so we may as well acknowledge them and learn to work with them. With increasing confidence and ownership of our core vulnerabilities, we may be willing to practice *kindness* to our fears. We begin to recognize that our refusal to participate in our disturbing feelings has generated the sense that they are external, alien things that are being done to us.

When we realize that our disturbance is us, it begins to make sense that being kind to what we don't want to feel is being kind to ourselves. Extending this realization, we practice *welcoming* our fears. We actively look for what we don't want to feel. We want to feel our shame, our rage, our grief, and our anxiety. Not because we like these feelings—we never will—but because we see that recovering experiential ownership of exactly what we had to disown as children will paradoxically cultivate both more aliveness and more safety. We practice trusting our ability to be just who we already are, rather than continuing our project of trying to be who we want to be or should be. In the next stage, we practice *committing* to our fears, challenging our hope that by doing this work, our core vulnerabilities will somehow be healed and go away. We commit to our disturbance as a valid part of our human lives, giving up our subtle fantasies of invulnerability, of a life without disturbance. As a next stage of our work, we are willing to practice actually *loving* our fears, just as a parent is hopefully able to hold their upset baby with the energy of unconditional love, even if they can't soothe their child. We can likewise hold our worst fears, open our heart, say "yes," engage fully, even while we wish things were different.

Each of these stages can be understood as an expression of our gradually increasing abilities and willingness to bring unconditional presence and kindness to whatever we may be experiencing at any moment. At first, we tend to apply this practice to specific issues we're having a hard time dealing with. As we progress, we may find that this unconditional acceptance and engagement is becoming an attitude just waiting for whatever may arise. Thoughts, feelings, fantasies, sensations—all continually come and go. Our attitude of unconditional kindness, though, is always present. As this experience becomes familiar and reliable, we may realize that we have *become*, most basically, *the activity of kindness*. What a relief, to be unconditionally kind to the messy, confused humans that we are, giving up any fantasy of resolving our worth or identity. We realize how exhausting it's been, feeling divided against ourselves, struggling for self-acceptance or enlightenment.

This path of dissolving our project of self-acceptance, of training ourselves into the experience of being most fundamentally the activity of kindness, is not the end of our work. We still have all of our neuroses, our conditioned history, and our lack of skillful means to work with. Western therapy has many great ways of working with these issues, and having given up our drama of being a divided problematic self, we can address all of these issues as practical concerns, not as evidence about our worth as a person. Imagine working with any of our familiar issues from the energy of unconditional kindness rather than attacking ourselves because of mistakes and limitations. If we are not a problem, then perhaps our issues are not problems—just patterns of experiencing that would probably be helpful to work with, both for our own benefit and the benefit of others.

Just as unconditional kindness supports our work with our relative conditioned issues, working with our relative conditioned experiencing turns out to support our practice of unconditional kindness. The better care we take of ourselves and the more skillfully we relate and communicate with others, the less unnecessary suffering and confusion we generate, and the less problematic we feel. It's easier to practice being kind to ourselves when we are engaging with our lives well. As we practice more sanity and less neurosis, our attention becomes less contracted and more expansive. It becomes likely that we will have more moments of awareness.

This is how I understand the work of therapy: to bring our relative experiencing into alignment with our current adult realities and current adult capacities, to deconstruct the variety of ways in which we continue to pretend to be problematic divided selves, and to open ourselves to an investigation into what is already and always most true in every moment. We discover that self-acceptance is a nonissue, but that cultivating a capacity for an unconditional accepting of all that arises in our awareness is a path that will continue as long as we live.

II

HELD, NOT HEALED:
THE JOY OF BEGINNING AGAIN

Jeff Foster

There is another way. It is the way of kindness,
the way of slowness, the way of true self-acceptance.

Falling in Love with Where You Are

Sometimes you just feel like a beginner, like you're back at square one. Yesterday, you were so clear, so light, so joyous, so at peace, so enlightened, and so totally accepting of yourself and everyone around you. You were "manifesting" perfectly, or so you thought, and your "vibrations" were high. You felt so free, so close to where you wanted to be, dancing and singing down the Yellow Brick Road of enlightenment; but now, all your evolution seems to have gone down the drain. You feel like a novice again, as if you've made no progress at all over the past few years or even decades, because unexpectedly a wave of sadness, or doubt, or anger, or fear, or longing for something you cannot even name has arisen. Something in your external life circumstances—at work, at home, at play, in relationship, in meditation, at the grocery store—triggered an old pain in you. A fierce doubt, an echo from childhood, a fear, a deep despair, a sense of abandonment, a loneliness, an uncomfortable energy you thought you'd already freed yourself from has returned. This is accompanied by tightness in the chest, a contracted feeling in the gut, a tension in the throat. Yesterday's clarity, yesterday's joy, yesterday's bliss, yesterday's self-acceptance seems so far away now. You feel like a baby again. Is this a mistake, a punishment? "I probably have done something wrong," you tell yourself. *Bad me. Guilty. Guilty. Wrong. Wrong. Wrong. Stupid. Stupid.* You start scrambling for solutions, answers, fixes, looking for some authority on this kind of thing, some sort of spiritual teaching . . .

It's amazing how quickly we blame ourselves, isn't it? How quickly we turn from the present moment, making it into a monster to be defeated or escaped, rather than a friend to be embraced, trusted, even loved. How quickly we assume that we have been kicked off our heroic path, and that the moment contains no intelligence at all.

No matter how evolved, awakened, or full of expertise we think we are, sometimes (if we're honest) we still find ourselves trying not to have the experience we're actually having, racing toward a different moment, a better moment, a more "spiritual" moment. *"This thought, this feeling, this urge, this impulse, this ache, this fear, this anger, this doubt, this tension . . . shouldn't be here!"* This is the voice behind all of our suffering. It is an old voice, a voice of fear, a voice of distrust of our own deepest experience. It didn't come naturally to us as children—we had to be taught to fear parts of ourselves, to run away from our embodied experience at a time when it needed our attention more than ever.

There is another way. It is the way of kindness, the way of slowness, the way of true self-acceptance. It is the way of staying close to yourself as you walk the path or get lost. Instead of running away from the present moment, can we slow down, and begin to face our pain, our discomfort, our fear, with courage and curiosity? Can we give ourselves permission to be beginners again, wide-eyed children, fascinated with our immediate embodied experience, wondering about our pain and discomfort rather than immediately distracting ourselves and disconnecting?

As Krishnamurti taught, when we turn away from our pain, suffering begins. We split ourselves in two. One part of us is *over here* in pain; another part wants to be *over there* out of pain. That is the real pain of life, dividing yourself like that, half in, half out, fragmenting yourself, rejecting where you are, and longing to be where you are not and cannot be right now. If we keep one foot in the present and another in the future, we lose our balance; we need both feet on the ground.

Seen through loving eyes, every moment is an invitation to let go of the image of how life "should" be, to let go of the hope that the moment is going to be any different, and to embrace the moment as it actually is. We bow to it, and honor its texture, shape, and taste, even if its taste is bitter. To accept means to take what is given, to receive what life offers. It's not about being passive; it's about aligning with the universe, cooperating with what it gives us in the present. We have to begin with the raw materials, the canvas of Now.

Sometimes what's given is our own inability to embrace the moment! So let's begin there. Let's begin by saying YES to our non-acceptance of the way things are right now, surrendering fully to our inability to surrender. Let's come into alignment with how life is actually moving in us. Let's tell the truth about our experience. This is not masochism, nor giving up on the possibility of change, but rather a cooperation with given energies, no longer being a victim of the moment but a willing explorer.

In my experience, when you finally say YES to the way things actually are, YES to the waves moving in you, YES to your fear and sorrow, YES to your doubts, YES to all the thoughts buzzing in your head, great change then becomes possible. You are clean again; you are whole. Something new can now emerge, out of the fertile ground, nurtured with your loving attention, your presence. Sometimes you have to stop pushing for change, and allow yourself to be pulled into the mystery of the moments for real change to begin.

True healing is not a destination, not about ridding yourself of pain, fear, sorrow, and all that, not about becoming perfect, or immune, or untouchable, but has something to do with saying YES to the present moment (the only moment we are ever truly in connection with), and affirming it, even if it is uncomfortable right now. Sometimes there is great intelligence in allowing yourself to actually feel worse right now, rather than scrambling to feel better immediately. To be curious about your symptoms rather than immediately rushing to get rid of them, remove them, numb them; for your symptoms may just be parts of you longing for love. Feeling worse, but consciously so. Bringing your precious attention (your most valuable resource) out of the past and future, and coming back to the living moment. Paying attention to the breath, body, sounds, and sensations of this moment. Feeling the belly rise and fall with each in- and out-breath. Noticing what it's like to be alive, here, on this day. Feeling the warmth of the sunlight on your face, hearing the sounds of the birds and the cars, seeing all the colors and shapes, delighting in the movement all around you, sensing all the energies moving in your body. This is true meditation: not seeking some altered state, or trying to reach some goal, but simply being awake to this precious moment, trusting the way of life—being *here*.

Letting Go of the Goals

Let me speak a little more about trust.

When you are watching a movie, and there is a scene in which the main character is full of distrust, pain, fear, anger, or deep longing for love, you don't think, "There's something wrong with this movie!" You don't think that the movie is broken. No, you trust that this scene is *part of* the movie. Even if you don't like the scene, even if it's a painful scene, or an intense scene that's hard to watch, you know somehow that it's not the wrong scene. The movie is not broken . . . even if the main character *feels* broken. Can we begin to trust our own scenes—our own present moments—the way we trust movie scenes? Who knows? Our painful scene, our scene of doubt or failure, even our scene of total breakdown, could be a huge turning point in the movie; it often is. It could be the scene with all the answers. We just don't know. The movie of our lives has not been written yet. It writes itself as it goes along. We just can't judge the scene as good or bad from where we are—the present scene.

You cannot escape the Now. Yet, as you've probably noticed over the years, you seem to spend a lot of time trying to escape the Now in various ways! With your brilliant and creative mind, you can rewind the movie of your life at will, conjuring up the past into the present, replaying old scenes; joyful scenes, upsetting scenes. You can fast-forward the movie, imagining the future—hoping, fantasizing, and even fearing future scenes. All of that activity is actually happening now, in the present scene, of course. You never actually leave the present scene at all; even if it's a scene of remembering the past or anticipating the future, it's still a present scene, still Now. You never actually enter the past or future at all. Past and future exist only as present thoughts, appearing in the current scene. You cannot actually be "out" of the Now.

Even though we are always *here*, and can't actually escape the Now, we always seem to be trying to get *there*. The mind will turn anything into a there. Healing, love, self-acceptance, peace, joy, Oneness, even spiritual enlightenment—the mind will make anything into a destination, a scene to reach, something that isn't here yet.

There is nothing wrong with imagining alternate scenes, of course; it's part of life too, a movement of great intelligence in itself. Yet, so quickly, in our attempts to get *there*, we start resisting *here*. We become so focused on what's missing, what's not here, what we *lack*.

The destination becomes far more important than the journey itself. The final step becomes far more important than the step we're taking . . . and this one . . . and this one. The present moment becomes an enemy, or a block, or an annoyance, or simply a means to an end, an insignificant slice of time. This resistance to the present moment, the disconnection with the present step, this *not wanting to be where we are*, this sense of lack, this focus on what we see as our lack of progress, goes to the root of all of our suffering. It goes to the root of our anxiety, our depression, our stress, and ultimately our addictive, self-destructive, and even suicidal urges. We disconnect from the ground, which is eternity itself, and become mesmerized by the shiny thing on the horizon, the Emerald City, with all its false hopes and promises. We make our peace, our happiness, dependent on *getting there*. We lose the simple joy of being *here*, being in contact with life.

When we are young, in so many ways we receive the message, "You're not enough." We're not good enough, attractive enough, fast enough, or clever enough. In so many ways we are taught to believe there's something broken in us, that we are incomplete as we are, that we must get *there* to have value and worth and take our place in the world. We shouldn't feel sad, fearful, angry, doubtful, and so on. Certain thoughts are wrong, bad, shameful, sick, and even evil. We are made to feel ashamed or guilty for having certain thoughts or feelings. Our experience is just not valid, or validated. "Cheer up," they say. "Get over it." "Stop being so afraid." "How dare you think that?" "You don't really feel that!" "You don't know what you're talking about!"

We carry that conditioning, that internal split, that mistrust of ourselves, with us into our adult lives, and often we don't examine it, we don't question it. Then, as adults, when certain feelings or thoughts arrive in our experience, we are still making them wrong, denying them, pushing them away, numbing them, and trying to escape. We may use alcohol or drugs to escape. We may work ourselves to the bone. We may give up on our passions and feel depressed and numb. We may even become spiritual seekers, and then the game continues. Certain thoughts or feelings are unspiritual, blocks to awakening, signs of ego, reminders of our spiritual failure, or too negative. The spiritual me wages war with the unspiritual me. We feel that we're failing if we're not feeling joyful all the time, peaceful, full of love, like those enlightened gurus (or so we imagine!). We compare ourselves to those seemingly perfect, awakened beings, and often feel so far away from them. We put so much pressure on ourselves, trying to follow the paths of others, mistrusting our own path. It all gets so exhausting, this war with ourselves, this constant comparison. We end up forgetting our true nature: presence itself.

You Are Presence Itself

We get so absorbed in the drama of our lives, we so forget the one essential thing, the unchanging background of our own living presence, without which the play of thought, sensation, feeling, sound, smell, is just not possible. It's like when you're watching a movie: you are so pulled into the drama, the time-bound movement, that you rarely notice the screen itself . . . well, unless it's a really bad movie! (As it happens, suffering or feeling that we're in a bad movie can be a great invitation to awaken—to discover that in us which does not suffer.)

What is your true nature? For what have you always been longing? To put it very simply: *You know you are alive. You know you exist.* You have always had this sense, deep down, of "I am," of being here, wherever you were. This sense of presence was there, shining brightly, when you were a child. It was your inner home. You didn't need any external confirmation. Nobody had to teach you. You just *knew.* You knew it before you could even speak or think. It came before words, before mind. It was there when you took your first breath—the most intimate and obvious thing. *You. Life. I am.* Throughout the joys and the sorrows, throughout the ecstatic highs and the terrible lows, throughout the intense and fiery experiences and the soft, loving, gentle ones, throughout all the seeking and suffering, you have been present, the one constant in your own life.

Even though no word can capture the boundless mystery of what you are, some people use the word awareness; some people use the word consciousness; some people use the word presence, spirit, god, space, emptiness, source, life . . . but in the end, the language we use really doesn't matter, and can just become yet another distraction. You exist before language, concepts, dreams, conclusions—before even the most beautiful and spiritual words like *awakening, enlightenment,* and *love.*

Don't go looking for yourself in the world of form. You already know who you are, and you have always known. What you are is not a passing state, not a specific feeling that comes and goes, not a transitory thought, not a specific experience, not something that arrives or leaves (for you cannot be present at the disappearance of presence). You are the vastness of sky in which all the fluffy and sometimes stormy clouds come and go, the room for every thought, every sensation, every sound, as they dance and subside, the space that holds, permeates, and ultimately *is,* whatever arises. It cannot be given to you; you are already That.

You are acceptance itself, the unconditional presence that effortlessly allows every thought and feeling—every pain, every joy, every feeling of nonacceptance or resistance, even the most fearful thought—to appear and disappear. All are welcome guests in you.

It's like every thought or feeling is a child at the door. The child is cold, starving, exhausted, and just longing to be allowed home, into the warmth of you. The child could be a feeling of sadness, fear, confusion, anger, or despair. It could be a thought, a troubling image in the mind, a dark impulse, or a strange urge. Whatever shape it takes, it is a part of you coming home, longing for your love. That child is here, not because you've done something wrong or you are far from healing, but because you are presence, the safety they seek, their true home.

Let's reframe the entire spiritual journey. You are never far from healing; healing is never a destination, or a place to get to in time. As presence, you allow all thoughts and feelings, however intense, however uncomfortable, to rest in your safe and loving embrace, to be held in your loving arms. This is healing, and it can only happen Now, *because there is only Now.*

Busting the Myth of Awakening

One of the biggest myths about spiritual awakening is that it is all about being perfect, getting into some kind of blissful state, where you're left untouched by the sorrows of being human. That's a misunderstanding of awakening, I think—that only the bliss and joy and warm, loving feelings will enter, only the well-mannered, well-behaved children will come to visit.

As presence, we know we are now the home for *all* our children: the bliss and the boredom alike, the joy and the sorrow, the certainty and the doubt. In the Bible, it is said that the divine "causes the sun to shine on the good and the evil alike." And so it is with the divine light of presence that we are; we shine on all our children, none excluded; all are lit up (or *en*lightened) by us. Our presence can hold them all. Our room is vast and loving. Our being is limitless. Our hearts are gigantic.

Over the past decade or so, since I first woke up to my spacious nature as presence itself, I've experienced all kinds of challenges in my personal life—physical discomfort and illness, the deaths of loved ones, relationship breakups, and my father getting diagnosed with

Alzheimer's disease. They've all been part of this incredible journey, and not mistakes, not errors, not punishments, not blocks to awakening, but portals to greater love. The journey with my father has been incredible and humbling—meeting him where he is, and as he is, as his whole conceptual world falls away, and allowing myself to meet myself as I am with him—staying present in the midst of heartbreak.

Becoming aware doesn't protect us from life, from pain, from discomfort. Not at all; in my experience, it is the complete opposite. Everything is more raw now. Every thought is more vibrant; every feeling is more dynamic. Sadness is sadder; it can finally be itself. Pain is more painful. Doubt is deep and sacred. When heartbreak comes, it is total, holy; it has been liberated to be fully itself. Everything amplifies itself because I'm not pushing it away anymore. I am no longer interested in numbing myself to life, pushing away these darling children of awareness and being some imagined perfect being. "Water that is too pure has no fish," as the Zen saying goes. I love my fish, those movements of my vulnerable humanity; I don't want to deny them oxygen any longer. I don't push away sorrow or fear; I breathe into it, dignify it, and bow to its sacredness.

There have been times—especially in the midst of intense physical pain—where I've completely forgotten the formless room of presence, and I've lost myself in the contents, the forms, so to speak. It seemed there was no space around the pain, and the mind just wanted out, dreaming of scary futures, longing to return to a peaceful past. That is suffering—forgetting your true nature as the vast room of presence, and going to war with the contents, identifying with something smaller than we are. I've come to see that even this forgetting is one of my children, and that sometimes we have to forget to remember. This is humbling stuff.

We can see failure not as pathology, but as path. Bowing before even my failure, letting my failure teach me humility and gratitude. I find nothing within me that is inherently unembraceable, no darkness, nothing against me or my path, nothing that is not a call for love and acceptance. Even failure is not to be feared. It can also be celebrated as part of life.

Say I'm sitting with my dear father, and I notice a wave of grief inside me. I don't turn away from it. I don't even try to work out why it is there, whether it's his or mine, or even what caused it. It doesn't matter. It's an old friend, come to me for healing, for holding, for love. To love my own grief is to love my father's grief and to love the grief of all my ancestors; it is to love the grief of all humanity, of all beings throughout time who have loved and lost and wondered why. If I turn away from this grief and pathologize it, I am turning away from *all* of life. I'm turning away from God. I'm turning away from compassion, from all those who grieve on this planet, from the universe itself, from the Big Bang, the dinosaurs, all the planets, the stars, the flowers, the future generations—the whole thing. Perhaps this grief is a language that we've never learned to speak—perhaps this grief is huge love in disguise; perhaps all feelings are. "I bow to you," I say. And I breathe into the grief, and it softens, becomes very tender, loving, saturated with presence, and I reconnect with my father again in the moment, even in the midst of grief. It's quite beautiful . . . the heart soft and tender.

Here is the invitation of every moment. A child arrives at the door, a pain, an old fear, a sorrow, a grief, an unexpected doubt, a "negative" thought, a scary picture in the mind, a raging loneliness, a sense of exquisite vulnerability, and it asks, "Will you let me in? Is there enough space for me?"

When it comes to love, you are always a beginner. That's wonderful. For love can only be known in the present moment—it is as fresh as the morning dew, as immediate as the sound of the rain falling on your roof in the evening, as pristine as the afternoon sunlight, unblemished by the passing of years.

Stop trying to accept, and simply see that your present experience has already been deeply accepted. Even your doubt, your confusion, your frustration, your overwhelm, your inability to accept or love or surrender, is holy here, deeply acceptable to life—a perfect expression of wholeness in itself.

It is okay; it really is. Even when it doesn't feel okay, it's okay.

Life is only a moment, so you can always begin.

12

WHAT IF THERE IS NOTHING WRONG?

Raphael Cushnir

When we're in the deepest, darkest, and worst emotional state, when it seems like self-acceptance is the farthest away, we are in fact one instant from the awareness that can transform us completely.

The hatred and cruelty we direct toward ourselves is usually rooted in two things: the brain's negative bias and early wounding. Here's how that works.

When our brain tries to protect us from what it thinks is wrong, either in the world or with us—but especially with us—this creates negative bias. We're constantly asking ourselves, "How am I doing?" and often this becomes, "How am I screwing up?" This negative shift is a function that evolved to keep us safe, to allow us to thrive, but in our society and the way that we've developed at this point in our history, it's in overdrive and mostly unhelpful. This internal feedback system evolved with a positive purpose—to tell us how and why we suck so that we can fix a problem so we'll be okay. If you were the slowest runner in your clan of cavemen, for example, you needed to recognize and correct that right away, or else you'd likely become a saber-toothed tiger's dinner. Negative bias is still perceived as a force for good, even though today it rarely is. We can never get off that hamster wheel. That's because it's not balanced by a part of our self that says, "Yay, you've finally gotten it right, and now I'm going to let up."

Negative bias works within us in a way that we can't control by simply fighting or trying to change it. Neuroscientists have spent a great deal of time studying and explaining the brain's negativity bias, but it is something that is easy to see in our daily lives even without neuroscience. When my stepdaughter was about six years old, we went on a vacation. I knew about negative bias, and I wanted to cement the positive aspect of the experience for her. I said to our gathered family, "Okay, everyone, we're going to go around the circle and say three things that we loved about our vacation." My stepdaughter went along with it and found three things to say. Then, as soon as we had gone around the circle, she rubbed her hands together with relish, had a devilish look on her face, and said, "Okay, now can we talk about three things that we hated about our vacation?" That always stuck with me because it shows we cannot defeat the negative bias by fighting against it.

What we *can* do is correct for bias. This means we recognize that we're going to tilt in the negative direction, and we can correct for it by adopting a clearer view that is probably more in the middle. It helps to balance the negative and the positive by putting a little bit of extra effort on the positive side. In that process, what happens is that we weaken the grip of the negative bias. It doesn't stop, but we're less led by it and much more able to adapt to it.

In my own life, I try to be sensitive to thinking and feeling, but also go beyond that to an energetic sensitivity. What I've come to recognize in myself is that when my negative bias is in operation, I get a "hunkered down" energy. As if a voice inside of me is saying, "It's wrong, it's bad." It feels like a dog gnawing on a bone. I'm highly attuned to that energetic state. Once I notice that it's present I can relax back into a broader awareness, or—with a sense of humor—I can let it run its course. I'll say to myself, "Okay, I'm the dog with the bone. Let me get this all out: let me gnaw until my jaw is tired, and then I'll relax back into awareness." Even when I let negative bias run, I don't believe it with the same intensity it had before I acknowledged it. It's important to have that awareness of what it feels like energetically in my whole being.

The other root of self-hatred and cruelty for most of us is early wounding. This means we didn't receive what we needed in terms of attachment and connection at some earlier point in our lives. At a very young age, when we're unconscious of this wounding, we develop one of a number of strategies to try to deal with the hurt, and in many cases, the trauma that lives within us. Our consciousness becomes organized in such a way that we try to avoid that feeling, so when it comes up, we get into a self-critical mode where it seems like we're feeling that feeling or we're coming from that place, but what's happening is that we're coming from our *resistance* to that place. The strategy becomes: "Do anything at all necessary not to feel what's in the core." Out of that avoidance comes what is often called "the trance of unworthiness"—the absence of self-acceptance. When we avoid our early wounds, we end up feeling worse, even though we think—consciously or unconsciously—that we're fixing the problem.

There are three basic ways to respond to negative bias and early wounding: collapsing, fighting or resisting, and neutral noticing. Let's look at them one at a time.

Collapsing into difficult emotions means aligning with them—as if they are the truth of who we are. We adopt a sense of, "Well, why fight it? It is the way that it is." We may believe that there's a positive aspect in this even though it's unpleasant, because at least we've stopped fighting the truth. Another way of looking at it is that when we collapse into negative self-belief and feeling, our awareness goes to sleep within that negative self-concept. Collapsing is often painful—why would we want to do it?

Fighting or resisting is the opposite of collapse. When we notice we have a self-critical thought, or when we feel unworthy and we start to shrink into ourselves, we're saying, "No! It's not good. I must develop positive self-esteem. I must learn not to judge myself." In that process, by fighting, we're colluding with the wound or bias. We think we're trying to fix it, but in fact, we're fueling the fire.

The third way to work with negative bias and early wounding is neutral noticing without engagement. It's thinking, "There's that negative thought," or "I'm starting to feel a collapse in my chest," or "My heart is breaking open," or "There's a hole in the center of my being." That sort of neutral response doesn't come naturally for us, but it is where the real positive shift occurs. The other two responses—collapsing and fighting—masquerade as being in our best interest or for our own good, but they don't have the conception of the fallout or endgame—they're perpetual.

As we grow to understand and identify collapsing into, fighting against, or noticing, we can recognize that there is an energetic posture that goes with each one. Collapsing into and fighting against are both straightforward—we're sinking *into* or resisting *against*. The key has to do more with the neutral state, because the term "noticing" needs some explanation. It's not just noticing in a clinical or analytical way—that's not so helpful in terms of self-acceptance. There has to be an element of caring—not fake or overly sweet caring, but a curiosity that comes from care. It's like when you love a young child and the child is having a hard time, so you want to know more about the situation in a way that is uplifting and supportive of returning the child to a place of knowing his or her own goodness and safety and being allowed to relax there. It's that caring curiosity that is the energy of the middle way—neutral noticing—which is necessary and can make all the difference.

To get to that place of noticing and caring and being curious about what we're feeling, we need to practice awareness, in general. Once we have awareness, we can shift the energy or the quality of that awareness. This works even at an intense or crisis level. For example, when I've worked with people who are in a full-blown panic state and have gone beyond "I screwed up" to "Get me to a hospital; I'm dying." How could they have any awareness in the middle of a crisis when everything is terrible? In those situations, my job as I see it, is to say, "Okay, right now in this moment you're having this panic. How is it manifesting for you? What are you noticing in this very moment?" That's when an instantaneous shift occurs, because the witness, as we understand from our spiritual traditions, never goes away even when it is obscured temporarily.

Most of the time, questioning what can be noticed in this very moment takes someone right back into the witness. If someone reports to me that it feels like his or her heart is pounding and they feel like they're dying, I might tell them to hold off on the dying part, because that's the interpretation. Instead, I'd encourage them to spend a few minutes with their pounding heart, their dizziness, and the tied-up-in-knots feeling in their stomach. What I often see is that a person shifts out of panic into experience held by awareness, which then brings up emotion. When a person connects to his or her emotion, they're no longer in panic. They can see the emotion that the panic obscured. If I point it out, they often say, "Yes, right now I'm desperately sad, but I'm not in panic."

That kind of example is about as intense as things get. In the middle of that intensity, I've seen how people can come right back to that witnessing place. Maybe the most heartening thing about it is that when we're in the deepest, darkest, and worst emotional state, when it seems like self-acceptance is the farthest away, we are in fact one instant from the awareness that can transform us completely.

This is not something I'd recommend doing alone. We can often only come to a place of greater awareness and peace through our connection with others. It doesn't always have to be a counselor; it can be anyone who can hold the space of compassionate presence for us. I believe in that space and believe that when we go into, "I must do it alone," or "I am alone," or "I have to pull myself up by my bootstraps," it can be debilitating. We need to be in connection.

That particular kind of connection only happens when we're with another person; yet it also helps reduce our feelings of negativity toward ourselves. Even without any advanced knowledge or special jargon, we all know that we're not skin-encapsulated beings. For example, when we walk into a room, and two people have had a fight and they're not even facing us, we may still know something's up. While it seems like we're constrained and confined by our physical space, even at a very young age, we come to be aware that isn't the case. Much of the time, we find ourselves in the space between—the inter-subjective. That's relevant because we often seek out people who are going to try to make us feel *better*. I don't think that's so helpful. It's helpful to seek out people who will support us in feeling *more*.

We need to reach out to people who really live and promote through their awareness the idea that there is nothing wrong—that there's nothing wrong with them and there's nothing wrong with us. That doesn't mean that there aren't issues in our own personal lives and in the world at large that need all kinds of attention to shift and change. It's not that. It's the state of an acceptance of what is *right now*. When you're sitting with someone who is exuding faith that there's nothing wrong with you—there's nothing wrong with you in the pain that you're experiencing, there's nothing wrong with you even in the self-criticism that's running through your mind—this is the thing that allows most of us to exhale. By contrast, if I try to get you to feel better, then I'm joining with you in a certain way in saying that there's something wrong with how you feel. If I try to cheer you up in an effort to rescue you from sadness, for example, and if I do this before you've actually felt that sadness to the extent that it needs to be felt, then we become inadvertent partners in resistance. Despite any short-term relief, the sadness remains repressed in your body. You pay the price for that repression until you're finally willing to release it.

In the throes of being unkind to ourselves, ask how we can reach out to other people in an effective way. I would use that as the barometer. I would notice how I feel around people that I'm connecting with when I'm in difficulty, whether they're professional or not. If they're giving me the sense that there's room for all of this upset, and yes, we can work on it, we can look at it together, but I'm fundamentally okay—that's the gold standard. That's what I would trust.

Once we get that, we also need to take what comes from the connection and begin to bring in what we've been temporarily outsourcing to that other person's holding and reflection. Strengthening our ability to hold our experience, whether we're beginners in the process or whether we're advanced practitioners, is always key, because even when we are far along the path, there are one or two or three emotional experiences in life that we still say "No" to because they overwhelm us or we haven't been able yet to say "Yes." We might want to, but we can't. To me, that is the essence of the healing path and even the spiritual journey: find those places inside of ourselves where we've said "No" and don't *try* to say "Yes." Cultivate a space of awareness in which we can hold them so that (even in the heat of it) we know the feelings are not who we are or what is defining us.

All of the things we're saying "No" to are in our bodies—so that's the somatic piece. There is nowhere else we're going to find them, because they arise as emotion and then, when we don't feel them, they don't go away; they stay in our bodies but become part of our unconscious trying to get our attention. As they're trying to get our attention, they're constantly met by the "no." The "no" is a physical contraction in our bodies—for me, my shoulders like to climb up around my ears; for someone else, it might be a tightening in the belly. We look for the physical contraction because the physical contraction is the telltale sign that a part of our brain that usually runs on automatic pilot has shut us down. Some call it "the primitive brain;" others call it "an amygdala hijack," but the point is that it's created an encasement around the difficult or painful feeling in our body.

The amazing and wonderful thing about this, even though it's very painful, is that when we bring this caring and curious attention to the actual physiological manifestation of an emotional contraction, it always opens. Because what's happening is that we're bringing a higher function to an automatic response, and that part of ourselves that creates the automatic response is super-powerful, but it also knows it's not the boss and that it has to listen. It stands back and says, "Oh, I don't know; what's going on here? I'm not sure I like this . . . okay, if you want to do that, if you want to bring your attention, I'll let that happen, and I reserve the right to shut down the show at any moment," but it still lets that happen. Then, we start having a different experience.

When we have a different experience, that part of us that creates the automatic shutdown updates and recognizes, "Oh, this isn't life threatening so I don't have to shut down like I did before." This happens in the body—the contraction arises in the body, and the release arises in the body. That's why it's so important when we're using this caring and curious attention to turn it to the experience in our body. It's not something our minds can get much traction with, and certainly when we try to change our external situation, we don't get much traction with that either. When we turn that attention to our body, that's where all the magic happens.

Sometimes when people are ill or they have something challenging going on with their health, that's one of the hardest times to work with this kind of attention and be kind to oneself. We feel like our body isn't there for us in the way that we want it to be, and we're not at our best. I have worked with challenging health issues throughout my life. For almost thirty years, I've had what is usually referred to as Chronic Fatigue Syndrome, which is a synonym for "We don't know exactly what's going on with you." It's something that I live with, and it shapes my functioning every day. It influences how much time I have to be in a high function—working and interacting with other people—and how much time I have to be either feeling bad or recovering.

The important piece about that is that most of us start with the idea that we're *supposed* to be in good health; our bodies are *supposed* to function in a way that either feels good or that we don't have to pay attention to because they're doing their thing so that we can put our attention elsewhere. When our bodies start to "fail" us, we come into the state that something is wrong. Sometimes it becomes self-blame: we've created this. Sometimes it becomes anger at God: why do I have to feel this way? The overall thing that unifies it is the idea that there is something wrong. Over the years, I've gotten more and more peaceful around my physical symptoms because I don't have an expectation or a need for my body to function in a particular way, so that when it's not functioning optimally, I'm not collapsing into or fighting it; I'm asking myself, what is available here? It all comes back to neutral noticing.

For example, I was giving some talks at a college, and it was a great group. I was excited to be there, but as a part of my physical symptoms, I had a terrible headache. For many people, the headache might be the kind of thing that would cause them to cancel the experience, but instead I chose to have an experience called "Wonderful Teaching at College with Terrible Headache." That's the way it was. It wasn't my preference to have it be that way, but I knew there was nothing I could do to change it. When something is wrong—especially when we're dealing with our bodies—we don't have to limit the ability with which we can care for ourselves and accept ourselves. Instead, that's where the greatest shift can be—we can go from frustration and lack of self-acceptance to, "Okay, what's the very best thing I can do to support myself in this very moment?" In the Wonderful Teaching at College with Terrible Headache example, it was to take the experience one moment at a time and to recognize that the headache was going to be present until it wasn't, and that gave me enough space to get through what I was there to do.

All of my emotional and spiritual healing work has led me to the crucial practice of what I call *surfing the sensations inside of our body*. In the worst situations or the most challenging ones, I come back to the two basic questions that set me to surfing. Those two questions are the synthesis of everything I've written about here:

"What is happening right now?"

"Can I be with it?"

The first question, "What is happening right now?" is so important because it's not *my* story about what's going to happen in five minutes if this headache doesn't go away, and it's not "What did I eat to bring about this headache?" Even though I don't add this to the sentence, what I'm really meaning is in my body. So, "What is happening right now?" This is an invitation to turn my attention to my body.

Once I notice what is happening, I ask the second of the two questions, which is, "Can I be with it?" That is to say, "Can I allow this to be exactly as it is, without interfering, and let it move and shift and change in whatever way it needs? Can I let it be, remaining caring and attentive, without trying to change it—or even to understand it?"

"Can I be with it?" is my core practice when I'm losing self-acceptance, when I'm in pain, or when I feel like something's wrong. It's also my core practice when I'm feeling awesome and wonderful. When I use that core practice in an expansive moment, it puts me deeper into connection with all that is, and it's the most freeing, peaceful, and joyful experience that I know.

13

MORE ON THE GPS FROM THE TWILIGHT ZONE

Geneen Roth

Being free takes first realizing you're in prison, and then questioning what imprisons you. Peace takes naming what keeps you ruffled. Joy takes realizing what separates you from it. It's a process, not a one-time event; you've got to want your life back more than you want anything.

In *Women, Food, and God,* I wrote a chapter called "The GPS from the Twilight Zone" in which I described the effects of self-judgment and how to disengage from it. In that book, I introduced what I termed "The Voice," the insidious inner critic that lives inside you and has the ability to usurp your power. I'd been working with The Voice for many years, and at the time of writing that book, I believed I had it handled. Turns out I was wrong.

It's difficult to convey the extent of the madness that ensues when I (or anyone) believe The Voice. The Voice can sound so dramatic, so extreme, and since I do tend to exaggerate a smidge—in writing (and in general)—you might think I exaggerate in the story I am about to share with you. That it can't be that bad. But there, you would be wrong.

A few months ago, I visited my friend Michael who'd just had his prostate removed, which meant he was bedridden with a catheter stuck up his penis and a urine bag attached to his hip. From his bed, he told me that because he'd been doing tai chi and chi gong for thirty years, he had just created a new kind of "laying-down tai chi," and was healing much faster than the doctor expected. Then he waved his hands gracefully a few times to demonstrate his magical moves. "You do look radiant for someone who's just had surgery," I said to him—and he did.

As my husband Matt and I were driving home, it started:

"I can't believe I didn't follow through with that chi gong practice. What is WRONG with me?"

"What if I have to have my ovaries removed and I don't know how to wave my hands over where they used to be and heal myself?"

"I KNEW I should have taken up tai chi thirty years ago when everyone was flying to Hawaii and studying with Al What's-His-Name. Now it's too late. I blew it. Again."

Along with—and even more pronounced than—the Greek chorus of judgments was the full-blown set of physical reactions that accompanied it: a pounding heart; a stomach that felt as if it had fallen through my feet and taken my legs with it; a sense of having withered and shrunk. Then came the wave of emotional reactions to the physical reactions: a feeling of irrevocable failure; desperation to climb out of myself; neediness for "a big person" to rescue the flailing me. And, as if that wasn't enough, reactions to the original judgments started piling up:

Look at you! You're such a fraud. You're supposed to be teaching other people how to disengage from this mess, and you can't even do it yourself. How many times, for how many years, are you going to have to keep going through this? Don't you ever learn?

Then, the final insult (which seems to be a favorite of The Voice, although it often has nothing to do with the situation-at-hand):

What a mess you are. You are going to die miserable and alone.

In the car, we were passing fields of grazing cows, humps of ochre hills dotted with wind-twisted shrubs and sprawling trees. Matt was burbling about how well Michael seemed and hadn't yet realized that she-who-had-woken-up-with-him, left the house with him, walked in Michael's door with him, had disappeared in a whorl of shame. When

I didn't respond to his attempts at conversation, he turned and said, "Are you okay, sweetheart?"

Silence.

The problem with engaging with The Voice—or any pattern that results in shame (and not all of them do; it depends on your proclivity to shame and the voices you've internalized over the years and whether they had a shaming element to them)—is that not only do you absolutely believe you are that which The Voice tells you, *but* you don't want anyone to know about it because you are convinced that if they saw the truth of you, they would be disgusted. Who, after all, could love a sniveling, worthless cockroach of a person? And because you hide what you believe to be your core self, any love you receive feels fake. It is as if you are pulling the wool over other people's eyes by hiding parts of yourself that The Voice tells you are you. You believe you are exactly what The Voice says you are—and so you hide. You become an imposter in your own life.

Matt was waiting for an answer. What I wanted to say was, "No, and would it be okay if I walked into your body now so that I could leave mine? And if that's not a possibility, would you mind telling me ten or a hundred reasons why you love me because I can't remember a single reason why you should."

"Honey," Matt said, "what's going on?"

I didn't have the courage to tell the truth, so I lied by omission. "Sorry," I answered. "Yes, Michael looked great and isn't the pink sky gorgeous and are we having poached salmon for dinner or did we decide on that zucchini frittata with chard from the garden."

By morning, I was still feeling small and needy and panicky—three telltale signs of the looming presence of The Voice. But because I hadn't yet recognized that the panic to be rescued was in direct proportion to The Voice's viciousness, I was awash in self-loathing.

Over breakfast of grilled cheese on sourdough toast with avocadoes and tomatoes, I murmured, "I should have taken tai chi years ago when everyone was doing it; I missed my chance." And Matt, having spent years listening to my proclamations of the life I could have had if only I hadn't been myself, responded, "Uh, isn't that your superego talking?"

"Hmm," I said, as if I'd never heard the word "superego." (Truly, The Voice and superego are one and the same.) I thought, "He loves me too much to see how damaged I am. Or else he's too lazy to get a divorce." But as I finished the last bite of avocado, I started feeling like Patty Duke playing Helen Keller.

In the movie *The Miracle Worker,* Annie Sullivan, Helen's teacher, refuses to let her leave the table until she understands the connection between the egg she is eating and the word for it. Despite Helen's tantrums, Annie persists with signing the word into her hand until finally Helen makes a connection between two things that were previously unrelated—and "a new light comes into her face." When Matt named the superego, I was able to see the connection between the doom and its cause; I saw that whenever the superego, or The Voice, is around, the needy panicky one is also around. They are a duo. And I suddenly understood there was another way to relate to my thoughts and the familiar emotional patterns they evoked. And—this was radical—I saw that they were actually just thought patterns and I didn't need to believe them.

It always feels the same, the turn that happens when I realize I've been in the thrall of the superego: as if an entity has been using my body as its host, but now I have a choice about whether to free myself from its clutches. "Really?" I think. "I'm allowed to do this? There is no prison, no door, no key? Really?" Seeing that I *can* free myself *is* freeing myself since the awareness that notices that the struggle is outside of it is, therefore, already free from it. And being on the other side of the superego (or, for that matter, any painful belief about myself, Matt, a friend, life itself) always, every single time, feels exultingly light—as if I've gone to the closet, put on the wings that were hanging beside my puffer coat, and am now soaring around treetops, shouting Hallelujah at every red-tailed hawk I pass.

* * *

It is important to note that each and every one of us has The Voice. And each and every one of us will be visited by The Voice at various points throughout our lives. We can be gentle with ourselves around the fact of The Voice, and we can be gentle with ourselves in learning how to work with it.

Each engagement with The Voice has recognizable ingredients: a big know-it-all bully wagging its finger at a small whimpering ghost child. It usually involves the following elements, although not always in this order:

The **trigger**, which can be anything at all: something someone says or does, a situation at work, an article you read about George Clooney or Oliver Sacks, a visit with a friend. You start comparing yourself to it/them/your own expectations of what you thought was going to happen and didn't. Or who you thought you were going to become and haven't.

The trigger is very personal and conditioned by your history and vulnerabilities (e.g., Matt did not respond to visiting Michael the way I did), and the trigger *does not have to do with the situation itself.* No one person or thing can cause you to devolve, shrink, or shame yourself; a trigger is created when you believe your thoughts and the feelings they evoke.

The **physical reaction** to the trigger: the pounding heart, the sinking chest, the feeling of shrinking to pint size, the sensation of energy draining from your body and leaving emptiness in its place, of being paralyzed or just too little to deal with this big bad world.

The **emotional reaction** (which is often simultaneous with the physical reaction): feeling small and/or young, abandoned and/or incapable, lost or unloved, doomed or dumb, isolated or valueless. Or all of the above. Although the trigger doesn't create particular thoughts or feelings or judgments, it does catalyze latent parts that have not been fully felt or understood. Everyone's got those parts—it's impossible to be born into this human, vulnerable body and escape unscathed—and until we meet them with compassion and openness, we are lived by them; they are who we take ourselves to be.

The **Voice/superego** (seemingly) comes to the rescue by telling you what you should or could have done to avoid feeling the way you are feeling now. Its main message is: "If only you had done that, then you wouldn't be feeling this." And: "There is only one way to live, and I know that way. You are doing it wrong." Unfortunately, we don't hear the judgments as if they are coming from the superego; we hear them in the first person as proclamations of truth, as if they are coming from a wiser, better, all-knowing part of ourselves:

- If I had taken tai chi, I wouldn't be feeling so afraid or doomed. And I could heal myself if I got cancer.

- If I hadn't decided to start my own business, I wouldn't be terrified of not having enough money now.

- If only I had lost ten pounds, I would be in a relationship now and not be so lonely.

In each of these circumstances, the superego is shouting an underlying, deeper criticism from the wings:

- You didn't take tai chi because you're lazy, and now your health will be ruined.

- You are worried about having enough money? Well, guess what? It serves you right for believing you could start your own business.

- You're fat because you are a sloth with no willpower; no wonder you're not in a relationship.

Ouch.

Engaging with The Voice is like mud wrestling with a pig, which never ends well, since the outcome is always the same: "You both get dirty and the pig likes it" (says George Bernard Shaw).

Over the years, I've tried and taught a variety of ways to work with the superego—defending myself by saying go away or fuck you to The Voice; listing its attacks by writing them down in the third person; thanking it for trying to protect me by shutting me down and, therefore, keeping me from making further mistakes. Some of these methods have helped here and there, but the only response that has ever truly worked is awareness itself: allowing myself to notice that I feel as if the ground has fallen away and I am living the wrong life. When I can bring this feeling of groundlessness into my awareness, even if it is days later, I can backtrack, name the trigger (what provoked the feeling of groundlessness), notice its accompanying sensations, and question the doom and thinking to which I've been wedded.

Byron Katie says, "I don't know what enlightenment is; I just know the difference between what hurts and what doesn't." Pounding hearts, losing the ground beneath you, feeling worthless and hurt. But—and here's the snafu—since most of us believe (and are afraid not to believe) the criticisms leveled at us from our superegos, we also believe that being loved and/or having the life we envision means obeying the One That Knows how to do it, have it, be it. So, although we may be peripherally aware that we feel as if we've shrunk, we are convinced that this-that-we-are-now is our true self, and we are back where we belong.

Disengaging from The Voice requires a willingness to consider that we've spent our lives hoodwinked by suffering—and that it's possible to be free. This, in turn, requires a willingness to see that what most people call "me-myself-I" ricochets from one insane voice in their heads to another.

Choosing not to believe the superego and the worthlessness that is its counterpart is like choosing not to diet; it's radical, frightening, exhilarating because, let's face it, it's comforting to have a voice in your head that is absolutely certain about what's wrong and what's right, what you need to do and eat to be loved, safe, and successful. As my teacher Jeanne said (and I've written before), we spend our life following instructions from people we wouldn't ask for street directions from today. And since most of us prefer to have company than be alone, we don't question our loyalty to their decades-old instructions or the fact that we often find ourselves wandering in the Twilight Zone of worthlessness and despair.

It takes courage to separate from The Voice because we're not sure who we would be on the other side. In the same way that we believe that without a strict diet, we would hunker on our couches, uncontrollably eating pizza and ice cream, we also believe (without knowing we believe) that we need the superego to keep us in line. Freeing yourself means stepping out of the status quo—the superego's job is to make sure you don't—and seeing that you are more than the sum total of your accomplishments, your relationships, your so-called failures, your body mass index, and your weight.

Being free takes first realizing you're in prison, and then questioning what imprisons you. Peace takes naming what keeps you ruffled. Joy takes realizing what separates you from it. It's a process, not a one-time event; you've got to want your life back more than you want anything. You've got to have a glimpse, a taste that you aren't who you thought you were (you're so much better)—and then, you've got to want that freedom so badly that you'll do whatever it takes, which is to question each time you start blaming yourself or anyone else (because the superego works both ways; it can either turn on you or someone who happens to be standing by).

And so, the two final elements in a superego skirmish, after the awareness, are naming and questioning the part of yourself you are now aligned with (your superego or its child counterpart) and inquiring into the validity of its beliefs:

- Is it true that I am lazy? What's the proof?

- Is it true that learning tai chi will save me from a horrible death by cancer I have not been, and may never be, diagnosed with? What's the proof? You seem to be forgetting the fact that although Michael knew tai chi, it didn't save him from prostate cancer.

- Is it true that my life is a mess because I gained ten pounds? Was my life better before I gained the weight or were my thighs just thinner? Didn't Jeremy/Jessica/ Aspirin-the-dog fall in love with me when I thought my thighs were too fat? Does Christie Brinkley really have a better life? How do you know? And by the way, if all those thin celebrities are so happy, why are they always in rehab, divorced, and/or killing themselves?

* Am I really the most screwed up person on the earth?

For some people, as I said at the beginning, saying "fuck off," "go away," or "go pick on someone who isn't lazy/has thin thighs," provides enough space to question the judgments. Some (like me) have to go through the process of shrinking and believing they shouldn't be allowed to take up space before they get fed up with the suffering. They have to want to be free more than they want to have company.

The last step is the **disengagement**—the wild joy that follows when you realize you've been caught and are now free, when you fling open the prison door, walk outside and gulp air and light for the first time in hours or days or weeks. Then you realize that instead of being either the bully or the child, you are the one who notices both. You sense what it feels like, who you were and what you knew before you defined things as good or bad, fat or thin, right or wrong. Before you became what you needed to be to be loved, you knew the holiness of trees and water and rocks. You knew the adults were a bit mad, but you loved them anyway. You had no doubt, not one, about who you were; you had wings, and now, you have them again.

awakening
SELF-ACCEPTANCE

14

NO STRANGERS IN THE HEART

Mark Nepo

Self-acceptance is a kind of courage—a quiet courage.
It means meeting life with who we are completely, being open to
how we're shaped in the same way the shore is shaped by the surf.

In the first half of life, I, like so many young people, struggled to find my uniqueness. What distinguished me from other people? How could I know that I was me? I tried to find my gift, and then I tried to stay devoted to it. As happens, life had other things to say—for me it was my cancer journey—but it can be anything. We don't need a life-threatening disease to show us who we are. It can be a sudden change in ambition. It can be the loss of a dream. It can be finding someone and then losing them. It can even be something unnamable, but eventually, we're all broken open.

In the second half of life, it turns around. Now I want to look for what I have in common with other living things. Paradoxically, it makes me accept and better understand who I am as an individual. In his poem "Driftwood," Henry Wadsworth Longfellow wrote, "If we could read the secret history of our enemies, we should find in each man's life sorrow and suffering enough to disarm all hostility." In other words, if we were to truly listen to our enemy's suffering, they would no longer be our enemy.

This speaks to the challenge to feel what life gives us *all the way through.* Often we feel it halfway. Because it can be painful, and difficult, and confusing, we often don't want to go there. It's only by going completely through our feelings that we reach that place where we know our whole self. Only from a complete sense of being, can we understand how we overlap with others.

We often feel separate from each other and ourselves. The great poet Rainer Maria Rilke has a profound line: "I am too alone in the world, and yet not alone enough to make every moment holy." I think we all experience this. When we hide in the pain of what happens to us, we remain in the limbo that Rilke speaks of. I've known this as a lifelong pattern—one that is common. When I am hurt, my reflex is to pull inside until I can get alone and figure out what happened. Then I can decide if it's safe to come back out. In that period of retreating, I am alone, but not alone enough to be connected to all of life. I am in-between.

When we're in-between, we're like a steel ball in a pinball machine, bouncing around and ducking holes. When we can feel what is ours to feel all the way through, we're not exempt from our feelings, but we have some grounding in the world's history of those feelings. This is why, when I feel a moment of love thoroughly, I am feeling everyone who has ever loved. If I am in a moment of pain and I meet it well, I feel the river of everyone who ever suffered. Going through any experience thoroughly—whether it be full of joy or suffering—deepens and reveals our compassion. Once we feel that deeply, not only are we aware that there are no strangers in the heart, but we also grow more vulnerable and stronger.

The road that deepens and brings us alive is crooked and winding, seldom straight. When I was recovering from rib surgery, I was told by wise nurses, who'd been helping people like me forever, that recovery was two steps forward, one step back. That turned out to be true. I think this makes sense for emotional and spiritual growth as well. I can lean into my shame or my fear, and then I'm going to recoil, because it gets difficult. That's okay. Lean back in. Take two steps forward, one step back.

Along the way, we're challenged to meet life on the surface while living in the deep. Think about the ocean. The ocean is surface and depth at the same time. The surface of the ocean may be churning and turbulent, and affected by weather, but below that—its depth—is unmoved. This is a way to understand our psychology and our spirituality.

Often we think, "I'd like to live just in the depth, thank you. That churned-up surface is just too much." Well, good luck. We can't do that. Nor can we live just on the surface. We are living all of it. It's understandable that I'm going to be churned up by experience, but when I can sink down and feel the depth beneath any one circumstance, I'm going to feel more connected to the ocean of all beings. That connection will enable me to be gentler and stronger. That's what I mean by feeling our way through—not escaping any one feeling, but feeling the total depth of it all.

Now, let's apply this to self-acceptance. To begin with, what do we mean by "self" and "acceptance"? When we talk about self, we're up on the surface—that's our particular personality and situation. When I can drop down to the depths of the sea under those waves of thought and emotion, then I'm in a place where my self connects with all Self. I think that's what meditation does. It allows us to be who we are in the context of all being. Every tradition has a name for this. It's *atman* in Hinduism, *dharma* in Buddhism, the Holy Ghost or the Holy Spirit in Christianity, and the indwelling presence of God in Judaism. When we disconnect from that deeper Self, it's a rougher, more turbulent ride. Accepting Self with a capital "S" means accepting the part of the Universe that resides in us, out of which our personality arises.

There's a distinction between striving for any type of perfection in life and what I call wholeheartedness. This brings us to something that is very difficult to accept, especially in our modern era, and that is—the acceptance of our *full* humanity. That means warts and all—our frustrations, our challenging traits, and our gifts.

Neil Douglas-Klotz wrote an amazing book, *Prayers of the Cosmos: Meditations on the Aramaic Words of Jesus*, in which he translated the teachings of Jesus from the original Aramaic. There are some profound discoveries there. For example, in the King James Version of the Bible, it's written that Jesus said, "Be you therefore perfect." Douglas-Klotz discovered the Aramaic was mistranslated and a truer rendition would be "Be you all-embracing." The original instruction from Jesus was to *be wholehearted.*

This mistranslation put a fork in the road of moral understanding for two thousand years. To be perfect and to be wholehearted are very different things. Being perfect has us exclude flaws and mistakes and try to hone our virtues to a point of pure living, which in my experience, is impossible and actually a dysfunctional way to try to live. Instead, being all-embracing or wholehearted means giving ourselves over to the entire incarnation of being human, something which no one can escape. It urges us to lean into life, to feel it all, to open our hearts enough that what comes in from the surface of our days mixes with the depth of who we are and continues to shape us. That's self-acceptance. It's a kind of courage—a quiet courage—to meet life with who we are completely, being open to how we're shaped in the same way the shore is shaped by the surf.

Even this metaphor fails, because we're human. We can't live in the depth. We have to come up to the surface and breathe. If we stay down there too long, we're going to drown. Every human being has to find a personal practice to determine his or her migration between depth and surface. We can look down there, but we can't live down there. We're creatures that cross depth and surface. Yet how do we live this openly? We have to enlist self-honesty if we're going to be able to do this. We need to know whether we're avoiding what we need, or whether we shouldn't go any deeper.

No one can do this alone. When confronted with aspects of who we are that we don't want to face, that's when we need friends. We need honest friends who say, "I know you don't want to do this, but I think you have to and I'll help you. Maybe you can help me when I face what I don't want to face." We need to face these depths because what's not integrated into our lives is repeated. That's another archetype. Ask yourself: *Am I moving closer to something through right timing, or am I simply in denial, avoiding the next doorway in my maturation of spirit?*

Along the way, I've discovered that the life of expression is part of the self-acceptance process. Through my cancer journey, I became less committed to the journey of writing as creating great art or products, and more committed to the expressive journey of healing. I began to understand that expression is a way to stay in conversation with our self and the journey of acceptance. Expression is a way to stay in conversation with our depth and our surface, and a way to uncover our personal practice of *being here*.

All this helps us to know our authentic center. The voice that comes from our authentic center is the tuning fork by which we realize the experience of Oneness. This is how we learn if we're close to what matters—when we feel that authentic hum in our heart. I know no other way to exercise that hum of Oneness other than to have an active life of expression. Writing is one of the closest and easiest ways to access our expression. Whether we ever show what we write or express to anyone, it's a way to evolve. The Sufis have a teaching about polishing the heart until it's a mirror of the world, and self-expression is one of the practices that does that.

Here's an exercise to try:

- Start by finding a quiet place and just be still. Then describe a time when you first had a sense of your own aliveness. Was that as a child? Was it in the playground? Was it first being with a friend? Was it your first experience of wind through your hair? What was it? Write a bit in your journal about that.

- Later—and I wouldn't do these at the same time—describe a time when you felt a moment where you were pulled away from that aliveness. Write about when something got in the way. Maybe it was a body image, maybe it was rejection, maybe it was a wounding parent, or maybe it was losing a job. Transparently enter and describe a time when you first felt disconnected from your own aliveness. What happened?

- Wait a week before engaging the third part of this exercise. Then, read what you wrote about aliveness and disconnection, and then consider what you've learned about the circumstances around knowing your aliveness and being pulled away from it. What can you learn about your own patterns?

- A week after that, sit down with a trusted friend or loved one and talk this over. Get somebody else's thoughts on it. See what you learn.

Early on, I didn't know to call this process of opening my heart "being a poet." It was just how I saw the world, and I knew my own aliveness by how the world spoke to me as a little boy. When alone, I felt an incredible sense of life that stood apart from the presence of others. I think this is typical of artists. When I entered grade school, I tried to share some of what I felt, and it wasn't received well. I was seen as peculiar, ignored, or dismissed. I felt muffled, and questioned my own experience. I think this a very ordinary occurrence, whether you're an artist or not. It gets to the heart of self-acceptance. There's a trade-off. We often find who we are in solitude, but then we want company. We're often challenged—do we give away who we are in order to belong? There's a constant need to balance solitude and community that engages us for the rest of our lives.

I struggled with wanting to belong well into my college years. It was very painful. On the one hand, I felt a definite connection to something in my life that was real, alive, and dynamic. Whenever I tried to connect with others about it, it didn't usually work. Finally, I started to have a few dear friends, so I didn't feel completely off the wall. That's when I realized if people truly love you, they want to understand who you are, and not prune who you are. It gave me the courage to keep putting out what my direct experience of life was and try to find relationship through that.

I think this is one of the problems of our age, and why we have so many kinds of fundamentalism. We have somehow adhered to the notion that we fear difference and variety, that we can only welcome sameness. The truth is, we need everybody's participation. We need each unique vision to create a living Universe that is whole. We hurt ourselves when we push people who are "not us" away.

This brings me to the word "genius." In our time, genius means a particular brilliance or a gift. Mozart was a genius. Einstein was a genius. Yet, I discovered that the original definition of genius was "attendant spirit." This is where the word "genie" comes from. Genius wasn't reserved for the particularly gifted individuals. Everyone has a genius. Everybody has an attendant spirit, a soul, atman, dharma, or whatever we want to call it. Self-acceptance has everything to do with staying in relationship with our attendant spirit, with our particular genius that helps us become who we are in the world.

I wrote this poem, "Breaking Surface," years ago for my students. I didn't realize it when I wrote it, but it's about the commitment to stay in relationship with our attendant spirit:

> Let no one keep you from your journey,
> no rabbi or priest, no mother
> who wants you to dig for treasures
> she misplaced, no father
> who won't let one life be enough,
> no lover who measures their worth
> by what you might give up,
> no voice that tells you in the night
> it can't be done.
>
> Let nothing dissuade you
> from seeing what you see
> or feeling the winds that make you
> want to dance alone
> or go where no one
> has yet to go.
>
> You are the only explorer.
> Your heart, the unreadable compass.

Your soul, the shore of a promise
too great to be ignored.

Ultimately, self-acceptance relates to the opening of the heart. It has to do with the long, hard journey of loving ourselves. We need to love that piece in us that has lived forever, listening to it, and letting it show itself despite those who say, "I don't understand," or "That scares me," or "Go away." We need to do this because being hidden from that Self creates a barrier between the world and the heart that is more damaging than any worldly rejection we could meet.

My cancer journey forced me into this level of open living. I have no choice but to lean into life and be fully here, which means meeting the world with my heart. I'm devoted to that without question or doubt. When each of us meets the world with that honest vulnerability, there are no strangers in the heart. This is our journey: to discover who we are so we can find that at heart we're all the same. Once we accept this archetypal deepening, we can discover that being alive is at once magnificent and beautifully ordinary.

15

TAKING IN THE GOOD

Rick Hanson

*The person to whom we have the highest moral
obligation is the one over whom we have the highest
influence, and that is our future self. So, if you want
to give yourself a gift tomorrow or next year, or
perhaps in the next lifetime, treat yourself well.*

I heard this saying from my Buddhist teachers: *The mind takes its
shape from whatever it rests upon.* An updated neuroscientific version, from the work of the psychologist Donald Hebb, would
be: *Neurons that fire together, wire together.* In other words, repeated
patterns of mental activity leave lasting traces in neural structure. You
have a choice. You cannot do anything about the brain you have in
this moment and all the things that happened in the past, but from
now on—three wonderfully optimistic words: *from now on*—you can
use your mind to change your brain for the better.

If we bring this understanding to the question of self-acceptance, it
means if you routinely rest your mind upon self-criticism, self-scorn,
self-scolding, perfectionism—in other words, stressful experiences
that are not self-acceptance—your brain over time will take a certain
shape in a sense, as it becomes increasingly reactive to negative experiences. For example, repeated release of the stress hormone cortisol will
sensitize the amygdala—the alarm bell of your brain—so it rings more
easily and more loudly; meanwhile, cortisol is over-stimulating and

even killing neurons in another part of your brain, the hippocampus, that puts things in perspective and calms down the alarm bell amygdala. In effect, changes in the structure and function of your nervous system are the lasting internalization of self-criticism, self-scolding, and self-shaming. On the other hand, if you routinely rest your mind upon realistic standards, recognize your accomplishments, internalize feelings of love and care from other people, and build up resources of self-nurturance, your brain will develop a different shape (in a sense), one that promotes more happiness, resilience, and self-worth.

There are three reasons why our brains wire in negative ways: we do or don't treat ourselves well; things happen to us; and our brain has what's called a negativity bias. When it comes to negative wiring, let's start with a line of inquiry from Tibetan Buddhism: *Is it given to you to avoid inheriting the results of your actions?* In other words, the person to whom we have the highest moral obligation is the one over whom we have the highest influence, and that is our future self. So, if you want to give yourself a gift tomorrow or next year, or perhaps in the next lifetime, treat yourself well.

The second reason is that things happen to us. We grew up in environments where parents are more or less affectionate, siblings are more or less critical, teachers and coaches are more or less supportive, and we have bosses, girlfriends, boyfriends, and friends. People influence us. We're profoundly social animals, and so there is an appropriate humility to respect the ways in which we are actually affected by the other people in our lives and the consequences of the ways they treat us.

The third reason our brains wire in negative ways is negativity bias—it's as if our brains operate as Velcro for the negative but Teflon for the positive. In other words, we have a brain that evolved to be very good at learning from bad experiences, but bad at learning from good experiences. We could have twenty successes in a day, accomplish twenty things, be praised twenty times, but if we have one goal we didn't meet or receive one criticism—*Boom!*—we remember that one.

How can we sensitize our brains for the good, becoming Velcro for the positive? We've all had the experience of something positive happening and knowing inside, "This one's a keeper. Let this one land."

Maybe we accomplished something or we're just very joyful, or we have some insight in therapy, or we're just standing under the stars and we say, "Okay, let this one sink in." That's how simple it is to take in the good. I've created four basic steps to help us do this. I call them HEAL:

- *Have it.* The first step is to have a positive experience in the first place. Either notice when you're experiencing something good instead of ignoring it, or create a positive experience.

- *Enrich it.* Stay with the positive experience for five, ten, twenty, thirty seconds in a row. Get those neurons really firing together so they really wire together by helping the experience be as intense as possible and opening to it in your body.

- *Absorb it.* Sense that the experience is sinking into you, like water into a sponge or like a jewel into the treasure chest of the heart.

- *Link it.* The fourth step is optional, but powerful. Hold both positive and negative material in awareness at once, but make the positive material more prominent, more in the foreground of awareness, bigger, so that it gradually associates with, soothes, and even eventually replaces that negative material. For example, while feeling cared about by a friend, you could also bring to awareness experiences from childhood in which you felt left out and unwanted.

These four steps may sound complicated, but in practice, they merge and the whole process usually takes one or two dozen seconds at most. We all know how to take in the good. I did not invent this, but I have tried to summarize the process—this fundamental neuropsychology of emotional learning—and apply it to particular issues. Like many other important aspects of human life, there has been little research on how to steepen the learning curve from beneficial experiences, which is what the HEAL process is about. For example, there is no exact right amount of time to hold a beneficial experience in awareness, or right amount of opening to it in your body. The more the better. The more times a day—five to ten seconds at a time, or longer—you actually internalize an experience of self-worth or self-acceptance, the better. The more intense these experiences are, the better. The longer they last—twenty seconds rather than ten seconds—and the more richly emotional and sensate they are, the better. All this said, keeping it simple, it really boils down to just four words: *Have It. Enjoy It!*

Many of our deepest experiences of self-criticism reach back into early childhood—the youngest layers of the strata of your psyche. If you are comfortable with the Link step of HEAL, it can be very powerful to connect beneficial experiences with negative material from childhood, reaching down to the tip of the root of your pain.

We should appreciate the power of everyday beneficial and typically enjoyable experiences. In fact, the enjoyment of an experience is usually a clue that it is beneficial, since our ancestors evolved reward systems to track those experiences that promoted survival and that passed on genes. These experiences *feel* good because they *are* good.

Unfortunately, so many of us deflect it when there's something good coming in; we brush it off. It's striking to realize how common this is, and often we don't notice these blocks to positive experiences until we deliberately try to take in the good. One block is that many people are just not in touch with themselves experientially; this matters because the point of taking in the good is to take in an *experience*. Perhaps they're afraid to get in touch with their own experience because for them, feeling their feelings is like popping open the trapdoor to hell. There are other reasons, too. People fear that if they take in the good they'll lose their edge, because when you start feeling good that's when you lower your guard and when life whacks you. Others feel that they don't deserve to feel good because they're ashamed of themselves, or they grew up in a culture where it was considered vain to focus on feeling good, or they have guilt, or whatever. Sometimes gender is involved: I've known women socialized to believe that their job was to make others feel good rather than put attention on whether they felt good; I've known men whose stance was to be a stoic warrior and feeling good is not part of the job description. Whatever the reason, it's quite helpful to examine if you have a block against taking in the good.

It is not selfish to take in the good. To quote Bertrand Russell, "The good life, as I conceive it, is a happy life. I do not mean that if you are good you will be happy; I mean that if you are happy you will be good." In other words, as much research has shown, when our cup runneth over, we're usually more inclined to be giving and helpful to other people.

Think of the brain as a garden. What can we do with this garden? There are three distinct ways to engage it—to practice with your mind. First, we can be with it without trying to change it, simply witnessing it. Second, we can pull weeds, reducing whatever creates suffering and harm for others and ourselves. And third, we can plant and grow flowers, growing positive factors—such as resilience, gratitude, and love—that promote the happiness and welfare of ourselves and others. All three ways to engage the mind are important—and we should be mindful during each one of them.

These three practices give you a natural trajectory for dealing with negative material, such as feelings of inadequacy or shame. For example, if I'm feeling bad, the first step is to witness the garden, to explore the feelings, the experience I'm having in an open, attentive way; accepting what's there, investigating it, trying to disentangle what's happening; seeing if there are younger, more vulnerable layers. At some point, it usually feels like time to shift into the second step and start pulling some weeds, releasing the painful emotions, the negative or catastrophizing thoughts, the tension in the body, and the self-doubts and worthlessness. After that, in the third step, I start replacing what I've released with its positive antidotes, such as taking in feelings of my own worth and the sense of being cared about by others, planting beautiful flowers in the garden of the mind.

In terms of these three ways to practice, to engage your mind, it helps to know what your strengths and weaknesses are. Personally, I was weak at the first step, and I wanted too quickly to make the pain go away and feel good again. I had to learn repeatedly that if you jump over the first step of fully experiencing the experience, it will catch up with you later. On the other hand, another person might just hang out in the pain a lot longer than they actually need to.

When you repeatedly take in the good—five seconds here, fifteen seconds there, a half dozen times a day—you naturally grow key psychological resources inside yourself, woven into your nervous system: inner strengths, like calm, contentment, and confidence. Growing these resources is like deepening the keel of the sailboat of your mind. Then you can dream bigger dreams and sail farther out into the dark blue sea. And when—not if—the storms of life blow, you're not so easily knocked over, and even if you get banged hard, you will recover more quickly.

When a storm does hit, my own personal mental first-aid kit has these four items in it:

- *Notice* when you're rattled—when the water gets choppy. Give words to the experiences, like anxious, irritated, or feeling bad. Studies have shown that the process of just noting with a simple word or label what we're experiencing lowers activation in the amygdala—alarm bell—in the brain. So just noticing you're upset and maybe even labeling the feelings can be helpful.

- *Self-compassion* is the second step. Compassion is the wish that a being not suffer, usually with a feeling of sympathetic concern; self-compassion simply applies this wish and sympathetic support to the being who wears your name tag. For me, self-compassion has a kind of sweetness to it: "Oh, ouch, I wish I didn't suffer. I wish that you, Rick, were not suffering here. Ouch, this hurts. I wish this didn't hurt." You are not resisting the pain or craving its absence, but simply bringing the same benevolence and concern to yourself that you would to anyone you care about.

- *Get on your own side.* I'm not against others, but I'm for myself. This is an incredibly important step, and one that many people don't have very well internalized. Be a friend to yourself.

- *Make a plan.* What are you going to do about this? Are you going to talk about it with your partner, let's say? Are you just going to let it go and move on? Whatever it is, make a plan.

The brain essentially has two settings; think of them as green and red. The green zone—I call it the *responsive* mode—is the default setting. It's where we go when we feel like our three core needs—safety, satisfaction, and connection, managed by avoiding harms, approaching rewards, and attaching to others—are fundamentally met. Then the body can conserve resources, recover from bursts of stress and repair itself, and refuel for future challenges. When we feel these core needs are met, the mind is colored, broadly, by a sense of peace, contentment, and love. This is the home base that has been developed by millions of years of evolution, which is certainly good news.

Then there's the red setting of the brain—I call it the *reactive* mode. This is the fight or flight or freeze reaction that kicks into gear whenever we experience that one of our fundamental needs—safety, satisfaction, connection—is *not* being met. In the red zone, bodily resources are typically burned faster than they're replenished; long-term projects in the body—like the immune system or digestion—are put on hold for the sake of immediate survival needs, and the mind is colored with a sense of fear, frustration, or heartache. This is what happens when you feel any sense of deficit or disturbance in your core, which is the neurobiological basis for the craving, broadly defined, that the Buddha pointed out in his Second Noble Truth as the primary source of suffering and harm.

The problem is that even though the green zone is our resting state, we are wired with tendencies and capabilities that make us quickly reactive in the red zone. That's why so many people are chronically stuck in what might be called the pink zone—they're experiencing chronic low-grade stress. If you look at humanity today, with seven billion people crowded together on one fragile planet, all too often caught up in fear, frustration, or heartache, you see that the brain's red zone is a major contributor to war, the greedy consumption of the earth's resources, and global warming.

Now, here's the thing: for the very first time in our tenure on Earth—150,000 years as our species, 2.5 million years as stone-tool manufacturing hominids—the objective conditions are present to truly make sure that every single human on the planet is reasonably safe, satisfied, and connected. We have the actual conditions that could enable the species to live in the green zone. This is unprecedented—this opportunity has developed in just our own generation, or at most, the one before it, but no sooner than that. What we do with this historically unprecedented opportunity—whether we truly develop a "green brain" culture worldwide—will be the defining story of the next century or two, and will determine whether our vulnerable planet and our children and their children have a softer landing than the one toward which they are currently hurtling.

16

TRANSFORMING SELF-CRITICISM INTO SELF-COMPASSION

Kelly McGonigal

When we are self-critical or experiencing shame, our sense of self becomes completely constricted around the part of us we feel has done wrong or is not enough.

As a scientist, I often wonder if some people are temperamentally born with a greater natural tendency toward self-criticism. I can't recall a time when that wasn't my primary orientation toward myself—the feeling that there was a big gap between whatever I was able to do or offer and what would be sufficient. I can remember failures going back as early as kindergarten. For years I'd believed that self-criticism was what pushed us, propelled us to success and self-improvement.

When I first came to the practices of meditation and yoga, I was introduced to the concept that relentless self-criticism is not necessarily healthy. I learned that it does not give us motivation. I began to get a sense there might be some other kind of motivation other than beating myself up. I wondered what that self-acceptance would feel like—being motivated by something other than the terror I might inflict on myself if I failed.

What I found was that if I stopped using anxiety or the threat of self-criticism as a motivator, a positive inducement emerged that was more connected to my actual values and aspirations. It felt different—more like a string tied to my heart that was pulling me forward, instead of that sense of being beaten from behind to keep going.

At first, this surprised me—that self-criticism might actually have been blinding me to a kind of intuition or inner wisdom that could point me in a better direction than self-criticism would. After years of personal exploration, academic study, and work as a neuroscientist and psychologist at Stanford University, I fell in love with the practices of self-compassion, not just for my own well-being, but also in teaching them to others.

Mindfulness was the buzz for a decade, but now it's compassion, and self-compassion, really. It's very hard to turn toward compassion without the foundation of mindfulness because compassion is about moving into suffering. When I started to teach compassion, people would come to the class, and as soon as they heard the word "suffering," their initial response was something like, "Oh, wait, I'm in the wrong class. I thought compassion was about love and just feeling good." I don't get that reaction quite as much anymore.

I don't know that there's been a global change and people are starting to turn toward compassion, or there's just so much suffering in the world that people feel they need skills to handle it in our society, in our communities, and even in how they relate to themselves. Either way, it's helpful to start with an understanding that all of our emotional responses are tied to survival instincts. It's important to recognize that everything—guilt, shame, and self-criticism—are related in a fundamental way to our desire to be close to and connected to others. We get angry so that we can defend ourselves. We get sad so that we can elicit social support from others. It seems like self-criticism and shame are instincts related to our desire to really fit into our tribe and be connected with others. We're even hard on our own self-harshness—we get so self-critical about our own self-criticism. The tendency to be hard on ourselves is about viewing ourselves from the perspective of other people or a community that matters to us. There is some seed of value in there, even though we often experience it as a form of self-inflicted suffering.

Another way to think about what's going on in the brain with self-criticism or emotions like guilt and shame, is that these can be responses to our own stress and suffering. This is different from the response we tend to have to somebody else's failures or stress or suffering. When we understand that, it's self-compassion.

When you look at compassion in the brain or you think about why it is that human beings evolved the ability to experience compassion, it seems to be an other-directed emotion. Compassion is an instinct that motivates us to help other people, even when the suffering is not our own. We have this whole other instinct for our own stress and suffering, which is more like the fight or flight response, or self-criticism.

These are two very different instincts, two very different ways to respond. Even if it's very easy for us to feel compassionate toward other people when they make a mistake or when they're in pain, when *we* make a mistake or hurt we unleash a whole other set of instincts—like shame, withdrawal, and avoidance—that is really about trying to protect ourselves from immediate pain or prevent future pain. It doesn't carry that same kind of natural forgiveness or natural tenderness that we often feel toward other people.

There's a reason for this. We're wired to be critical of ourselves and compassionate toward others because we want to be accepted by the group. *However, we're not wired—it is not in our nature—to be compassionate toward ourselves.* Fortunately, we can always do more with what we have than what our natural tendencies are. Self-compassion—and likewise self-acceptance—is an evolutionary development that's in progress. We are in a place where we're beginning to experience the unnecessary suffering that comes from giving in to the tendency to be so self-critical.

We have such a strong innate tendency to respond to our own pain and suffering with fight or flight, stress, or a sense of "I have to fix this now," and those responses include self-criticism. The ideas of being hard on ourselves, of wanting to punish ourselves, or wanting to stop ourselves are all related to that kind of stress instinct, which is our strongest survival instinct when it comes to our own challenges. Science can't yet tell us why our self-defense instincts are more fear-based than nurturing; we just seem to be wired that way. Even our most pro-social instincts can push us toward shame. The desire to be a good member of our "tribe" can lead to disappointment, self-doubt, and even self-hate when we feel that we have let others down or are inadequate in any way.

The trick is to learn to have a relationship with ourselves wherein our natural compassion instinct can be turned toward ourselves. It's a very interesting dilemma because we have to not only *be* the one who is suffering, but we also have to find the part of ourselves who can witness the one who is suffering and have a relationship with the one who is suffering. In other words, to become self-compassionate, we have to be both the self who is feeling bad or in pain or made a mistake, and the self who is holding that suffering.

Usually what happens when we are self-critical or experiencing shame is that our sense of self becomes completely constricted around the part of us we feel has done wrong or is not enough, or whatever it is that created the bad feelings. In the compassion cultivation courses I teach, we have several different types of practices to help reorient compassion for others toward ourselves.

The first practice is a basic self-compassion meditation. You begin by trying to touch the part of yourself that feels compassion for somebody else's pain or somebody else's failures. Perhaps you begin with a loved one, a child, a pet, a family member, a partner, and you notice how easily you can feel for and still see the good in your loved one despite their mistake or stress. Then, you take that feeling into your body—you take that emotion and you turn it toward your own stress, your own failures. It's a very traditional meditation practice.

Early in my life, I experienced chronic pain. I realized that part of my self-criticism, and the sense of disconnection or self-rejection that comes with it, was directed at my body. As a result, I created a second practice I call "befriending the body." You simply put a hand somewhere on your body, often where you can feel the breath. In your mind, think something like, "Thank you body, for working so hard. Thank you body, for never abandoning me." That's a practice that instantly changes the relationship I'm having with the part of me that I have the most experience rejecting.

If you're experiencing another form of self-criticism—something like self-doubt or regret—you can try a practice where you think about all of the other people who might also be experiencing that particular feeling. Maybe I'm feeling bad about letting someone down, so I might bring to my consciousness, "Right now there are countless parents who feel that they've let their children down. There are countless people who feel that they are letting people down financially because they don't have the resources to keep people employed. There are so many people all over the world who know this flavor of real sadness and regret for not being able to actually offer what they want to offer." Whatever the particular content is, I try to think about it from the perspective of common humanity. This allows me to have a relationship with myself instead of feeling so sucked into, "This is only me. I am uniquely screwed up and inadequate," or whatever my inner self-critic would have me believe.

A final practice is a letter-writing practice. I encourage people to write letters to themselves from different aspects of themselves, to try to get at how they can build a relationship with the self who is suffering, the self who they typically criticize. You could write a letter to your suffering self from your wiser self. You could also write a letter to your present suffering self from your wiser future self: somebody who can really see the big picture of how what's happening now might fit into the trajectory of your life. It's a way to see your own strength and the possibility that is still present, and to really zoom out in time to reveal the big-picture point of view. A twenty-five-year-old can seem very wise when you're eighteen. If you're forty, maybe you want to go to sixty or seventy. It could even just be next week. The idea is that there is going to be a version of you who can look back at where you are now with gratitude and appreciation for what you are going through in the present.

I've spent a lot of time considering habits and willpower and how they relate to self-acceptance. Our habits have so much momentum behind them that we're often convinced that the only way to interrupt a pattern—say, the avoidance, withdrawal, or self-sabotage rooted in anxiety and self-criticism, or self-destructive behaviors like overeating and addiction—is to get rid of the inner experiences behind them. Often people think they need to stop the inner experience—not think about the worry, not feel the emotion, not have the craving, not have any self-doubt—but mental and emotional habits have tremendous momentum. When they arise, they are moving through us. If we try to get in the way—to suppress the feeling, argue with the thought, or push an impulse down—it is like trying to get in the way of a giant truck. We're going to be run over by it. This paves the road for self-criticism.

What I recommend for all habits, but especially for mental habits, is to start by bringing compassionate awareness to them. The way to start developing compassionate awareness is with the breath and the body. Whether I'm working with people who are dealing with will-power challenges—it could be addiction, not just mental habits—or whether we are doing compassion training, we always start by cultivating compassionate awareness of the breath.

There's a way of paying attention to what's happening that is simply acceptance. Once you have that ability to attend to the breath in that way, you can often turn it toward the mental habit that you're trying to change. That first step is *the* critical first step for changing a mental habit. Everything else after that, it's just fun.

The next step in developing compassionate awareness is to intentionally invite in the opposite of the habit. That could be self-appreciation. Every time there is an influx of self-criticism, we need to remind ourselves of a value that we care about and something we appreciate about ourselves, or remember something we did that was consistent with one of our values. It doesn't have to feel balanced. I really think that transforming habits is about working in small increments, and each small change makes the scale a little less tilted. That process brings a lot of transformation over time.

I define willpower as the ability to do what matters most to you, even when it's difficult. I feel that's a perfect description of what it is we're actually doing when we try to work with self-criticism and invite in self-compassion. Your willpower challenge might be trying to resist a temptation—like junk food, a cigarette, or spending money—or trying to find the strength to do something that makes you anxious, that fills you with self-doubt, or that makes you physically uncomfortable. Whatever it is, it's a matter of accepting that there's going to be some voice in your head that is going to be resistant, or there might be sensations going on in your body that are difficult to be with, just like with self-criticism. It's also about being able to remember what your intention is and that some part of you is going to be able to hold the big picture in mind and point you toward your goals and toward values and positive actions. Willpower is a very compassionate way to release self-criticism and relate to ourselves.

Some people seem to be higher on the self-critical self-rating scale. There is not a great deal of research on the neuroscience of self-criticism, but there is some research on things that are related. One of these is the big difference in the degree to which individuals are "approach motivated" versus "avoidance motivated." These motivations seem to be represented by differences in activation in the right and the left sides of the prefrontal cortex—people have differing degrees of symmetry or asymmetry. Those who have greater general activity in the right side of the prefrontal cortex tend to be more motivated by avoiding bad things than they are motivated by going after positive things.

This is true of my temperament—I'm a right side of the prefrontal cortex person. Since childhood, if anyone has wanted me to do something, all they need to do is threaten punishment, letting people down, or physical pain. *That* is like plugging me into a wall. *Boom! Charge!* You got me. The promise that I might earn a reward is less electrifying and less likely to switch on my motivation.

My guess is that individual difference, whether we are oriented toward chasing what we want or avoiding what we don't want, may have to do with why people vary in their self-criticism and self-acceptance. In my experience, there's a higher correlation between self-criticism and sensitivity to stress.

No amount of meditation or positive thinking is going to completely change someone into a person who is primarily motivated by chasing prizes or primarily motivated by fear. That is probably never going to happen, but what we cultivate is much more willingness to tolerate and work with our discomfort. People often show up to psychological practices or to a spiritual path after a difficult experience. I think that as people suffer, they look for the tools to deal with that suffering. Self-compassion and compassion for others is a good place to find that.

17

PERFECT IN OUR IMPERFECTION

Colin Tipping

That is really what radical forgiveness is all about—that people can feel better about themselves, accept themselves, love themselves more, and know that they are perfect just the way they are.

The challenge of self-acceptance and self-forgiveness is something I've delved into quite deeply in my work. Self-acceptance is a question of underlying beliefs—what we think of as our own self-concept—and trying to discover what they are and how we can neutralize the negative ones so that they stop affecting us. We really do need help when it comes to the self-acceptance issues.

There's no question that guilt and shame are the two emotions most attached to our need for self-forgiveness and self-acceptance. It's important to make a distinction between guilt and shame. Guilt is about our behavior—it's about what we have done and feel guilty about, or haven't done and should have. Shame is about who we think we are: *I'm a bad person. I'm unlovable. I'll never make it. I'm just not good enough.* That's really shame. What we know about both of these emotions is that once we go there, it's hard to lift ourselves out of them.

According to psychiatrist David Hawkins, guilt and shame are at the lowest vibration on his human personality scale, which ranges from the primitive at zero to enlightenment at one thousand:

20	Shame
30	Guilt
50	Apathy
75	Grief
100	Fear
125	Desire
150	Anger
175	Pride
200	Courage
250	Neutrality
310	Willingness
350	Acceptance
400	Reason
500	Love
540	Joy
600	Peace
700–1000	Enlightenment

Shame and guilt are at the very bottom, at twenty and thirty. They're even lower than anger. According to Hawkins, anger is at a higher level because when we get angry we are spurred into action—we make things happen, we do something about what's making us angry. On the scale, after shame and guilt comes apathy. If we're ashamed, then it's very hard for us to get out of this state because we're apathetic about it. We have bought into negative beliefs—we are no good; we are unlovable; we are not good enough—and so we have reached a point where we need help.

When I work with people who are suffering with shame, the first thing I do is identify that feeling and allow them have it, allow them to express it. That's where we start, no matter what the feelings are. I let them talk about their shame; I let them talk about their guilt—or whatever emotion is arising.

From there, through the process of *radical forgiveness*, we can undo some of the unconscious beliefs that give rise to and support the negative feeling that is troubling them. The first thing I need to know when I work with someone on guilt and shame, or any kind of difficult emotion, is that they have some understanding of what radical forgiveness is and the paradigm on which it is built. Radical forgiveness is very different from conventional forgiveness.

The principle underlying radical forgiveness and radical self-forgiveness is that we create everything that we need for our soul's growth—there are no accidents; there are no mistakes. Nothing wrong is actually happening because it's what our soul wanted to experience, so the event that's occurring for us is actually something that we have created, or co-created with other people or other souls through a soul contract (I'll explain more about this later). Therefore, there is nothing to forgive. That's it in a nutshell, but if you try to explain that to somebody who is suffering terrible guilt and shame—it's very, very difficult. You have to gentle them into the whole idea that there is a certain perfection in what is occurring to them. It can be a perpetrator's story or a victim's story, but either way the story is making them feel bad.

Radical forgiveness is a straightforward technique as long as you have sensitivity to how and when you present it to a person who's in pain—and that's the key to good coaching or good counseling. The tools and the actual process are very simple, very easy, and anybody can do them. It doesn't require any belief. It doesn't require more than a modicum of intelligence, special skills, or anything. It is available to virtually anybody. With conventional forgiveness, most people feel that they pretty much have to be a saint to be able to do it; only special people actually end up fully forgiving, and the measure of that is that they usually end up on *Oprah*.

There are fives stages of radical forgiveness:

- Telling the story
- Feeling the feelings
- Collapsing the story
- Reframing the story
- Integrating the new story

First, a person must tell their story. If someone comes to me and they're in a bad state because they're feeling shameful or guilty, I want them to talk about it. I want them to tell me how they're feeling, what the story is, what has made them feel this way. That's of paramount importance and sometimes it takes two sessions just to get through that.

Second, the person needs to feel the feelings associated with their story. This is essential. Then, they can begin to collapse the story by removing all the stuff they've made up that is completely not true, such as their judgments, their expectations, or assumptions they might have made.

One of the things we have to ask ourselves about guilt is, is it appropriate or not appropriate? Am I entitled to feel guilty or not? In many cases, people are *not* entitled to feel guilt. They didn't earn the right to feel guilty because they weren't in any way complicit—they were not at fault—but they've taken on the guilt anyway because of the situation. In many instances, if we find it's inappropriate, that's almost the end of the story, but not always.

The fourth step, after collapsing the story, is to reframe that story. That's when we go to the metaphysical principles underlying radical forgiveness and radical self-forgiveness: that nothing wrong is happening, and therefore there's nothing to forgive. It's very hard for people to get that at the mental level. In fact, it's a crazy idea. The mind simply rejects it, which is why I've created a series of worksheets to help people to bypass the mental mind and allow the spiritual part of our mind to work on it energetically—I call that *spiritual intelligence*.

Finally, we integrate the story into the physical body. With guilt and shame, they are such low-vibration emotions that it's hard to lift somebody out of them quickly. Sometimes it might take several sessions to bring people to the point where they are willing—and willingness is all that is required—to get where they're able to see that nothing wrong actually happened and that at the spiritual level it was all part of a divine plan. Even if what they did deserved guilt or was wrong at the *human* level, in spiritual terms there was a purpose there; it was meant to happen that way.

It takes some time to learn how to reframe a story. We can't just jump in and say, "Oh, it's perfect the way it is." We can't say that to somebody who, for example, has been sexually abused. It's not an intervention technique. It's something that we gradually open for people—the possibility that there is another way to look at an experience. You're probably entitled to guilt if you got drunk and caused a car accident—you're entitled to feel guilty about that because you did wrong at the human level. But maybe there was some reason why that had to happen, some lesson that you had to learn, something that the other person needed to learn. Maybe there was some sort of divine purpose in it, which we might never know. It's not that we have to figure it out. All we need to do is to be open to the possibility there may be a purpose behind our guilt or shame that is beyond our comprehension, but is spiritual nevertheless.

The only reason that I can say radical forgiveness is worthwhile is because over the twenty years we've been doing it, it seems to have an immediate effect on people energetically. Their spirits lift; their vibrations go up a little bit so that they can move to the next level on Hawkins's scale of vibration, and they find a level of peace that they would not find using conventional therapy or conventional forgiveness. In my experience, the effect is immediate.

In my work on self-forgiveness, the two areas where I see people suffering the most shame are finances and body image. Money has so much meaning in our culture, about self-worth, status, who we are, and what value we put on ourselves. It all has a tremendous amount of meaning, and we learn very early in our lives how we should interpret this meaning for ourselves relative to how we were brought up, the social class we were born into, and the people who surround us.

The challenge many people encounter is the self-judgment that can come when our financial situation does not measure up to what we think it should be. All of the beliefs we have around money become part of our identities. Let's say we've come from a very poor family and we believe that's how it is for us people, then we'll always be poor because that's the belief that we hold. It is all a question of belief: identifying those beliefs, discovering what they are, systematically undoing those beliefs once we have discovered what they are, and then transforming them to support us as we move into a different, higher vibration, so that we can attract money or abundance.

We don't have to go back very far to remember some of the ideas that we were fed when we were small, the most common of which are ones like: *Money doesn't grow on trees. You think you can have all you want? Well you can't—it's in short supply. There's not enough to go around. Some people have money, some people don't—that's just the way it is.* Alternatively, if you were born into a social class that wasn't used to being rich, then money may become suspect.

When I grew up, I heard my family and people in my milieu say things like, "You know, if you're rich you must've got it because you're a criminal. Rich people are bad people and they probably got it through bad means. You can't trust people with a lot of money. Money causes an awful lot of pain and anguish." All of those beliefs are discoverable if you work through them and look hard at your relationship with money.

One of the ways to discover any kind of belief, whether it's about self-acceptance or worth, is to look at what is showing up in your life. If money is continually drifting away from you, or not coming in, then there is absolutely a belief that money should not come to you. This is because we create our reality—we create everything in our lives moment by moment. Whatever is showing up in your life is showing you what your beliefs are. So if you're constantly short of money, then there's part of you that believes you're not entitled to it, that you're not worthy of it, or that money doesn't come easily to you.

Another way to see what your beliefs are—about money or about yourself or about any aspect of your self-concept—is to ask: Who is it out there who I judge severely for being a certain way? In other words, who am I projecting my beliefs onto that is making me become upset or self-righteous? That will show you what your beliefs are because we project our subconscious beliefs onto other people and make *them* wrong, or judge them for having those beliefs. Sometimes it's the other way around—or the reverse of those beliefs. Those we judge and whatever we judge them for become a mirror for what our beliefs are—and that's one of the primary ways to discover them. Once we know our beliefs, we can start the work of neutralizing them and transforming them.

Body awareness is another huge example. We know that society promotes an illusory form of the ideal body—especially for women.

This has caused an awful lot of people to feel bad and to form a self-image that is not the truth, because you very seldom meet anyone who is satisfied with their body. It's not just obese people who are dissatisfied with their bodies. Most people would rather be different from the way they are in some way or another.

I have a metaphysical, esoteric explanation for this. We came into this life experience as a spirit, as a soul, and one of the things we had to do was to lower our vibration enough to create and inhabit a body so that we can experience the idea of being separate, as opposed to being part of the All That Is. However, our bodies are very heavy items to have to carry around and they often let us down. I think there might be part of us that really resents having to have this body, and that we have a hard time accepting it simply because we'd rather not have one at all. We'd rather go back to being just a spirit without a body and being who we are in truth, as opposed to the illusion that we're separate from the All That Is and in a body. It's almost like we come to this life with a built-in resistance to having a body, and we project a lot of our feelings and dissatisfactions onto that body, creating ill health, obesity, and all sorts of other things to project our discomfort with being in the physical world and in a body. What that reason is, we really don't know, and it really doesn't matter. We can simply embrace perfection as a possibility and see if it works.

In my metaphysical view, people might be relating to their bodies with, "Oh, I resent the fact that I'm not pure spirit." Why is it that even people who have lovely bodies are still dissatisfied? What's the underlying dynamic that would make people feel so unhappy with their bodies? This occurred to me when I was writing my book *Radical Manifestation*, which has a whole section on body awareness and weight issues. Perhaps we have this in-built resistance to having to haul this thing—our body—around for upward of seventy years.

My test for radical forgiveness is simple: Does it work? The answer is yes, it does. For the last twenty years, I've seen it succeed many times. The transformation is profound. It is not important whether the theory that I use is correct or not. It works well enough to be able to teach other people how to do it and how to give the tools to other people to help *them* do it.

When we open our minds to this possibility of radical forgiveness, something happens to us, something clicks. Something deep within us recognizes that truth—we immediately feel better, and we begin the healing process. That is really what radical forgiveness is all about—that people can feel better about themselves, accept themselves, love themselves more, and know that they are perfect just the way they are.

We are perfect in our imperfection, and without that imperfection, there would be no opportunity for the soul to grow and learn and for us to engage in the learning and growing of every person on the planet. It is all part of something much, much larger than we are, something that we don't understand because we don't have the consciousness to really grasp it. All we can do is our best to bring people to awareness that there's more to this life than just what we register with our five senses. There is a spiritual reality beneath the surface, and even though we don't know what it is, we can recognize that it's there and work with it the best we can.

Engaging in radical forgiveness and self-forgiveness doesn't involve a belief of any kind. I always say, "I don't believe this, but I make certain assumptions." There's a big difference between an assumption and a belief. An assumption is always there to be challenged and to be revised if some evidence to the contrary comes up. A belief is a much-hardened system that puts us in a box, which we then have to defend, because if I believe something I have to stand by it; I have to believe it; I have to make arguments for it in order to convince other people.

If I make an assumption, I may be right; I may be wrong. I don't really care very much about it. If I'm making a wrong assumption, fine. Show me a better one. It's always contingent, and I think one of the things that people say about my work with radical forgiveness is that I'm not adamant about it, that it's always contingent upon how we interpret these things and the stories we make up about them. That's why I say I don't *believe* in radical forgiveness. If it didn't work, I would drop it immediately because I have no commitment to a belief system around it. I make up a story, which I think supports my assumptions of why it works, but I have no attachment to that story or to those assumptions. If they're wrong, they're wrong. If they don't work anymore—if the tools I've built around these assumptions don't work anymore—I'll drop them.

Of course, there are a whole set of assumptions that support my worldview. The worldview is that we work in two dimensions simultaneously. One is the physical plane, and the other plane is where we go to experience the lessons that teach us what oneness really is through the pain of separation. When we're working with the spiritual realm at the same time that we're living in the human realm, it's possible for us to be cognizant of both at the same time and to be effective on both planes simultaneously.

The spiritual world or spiritual realm that I'm talking about is where there is no such thing as death. Again, that's an assumption I make, that we are who we are before we came in and took on a body, and that when we drop that body we'll be the same entity that we were before. In my opinion, we're immortal—we don't die. We simply make a transition from one vibration to another.

Another assumption I make is that we have a soul contract or a plan that we have created with other souls before this incarnation. We agreed to do certain things to and for each other in order to be able to experience what it is we came to this life to experience according to our karma. There are many assumptions built into my particular worldview, but I'm not locked into any of it because it's not a belief system. It's not dogma. It's not a religion. I make a very clear distinction between religion and spirituality. The assumptions I make seem to support the work that I do and allow people to heal or to grow and learn in the way that they want to, so I'll hang on to them until I hear otherwise.

All we need to know is that whatever is occurring in our life has a purpose to it and is meant to happen. We're not privy to what this bigger purpose is for our human journey, but we're taking this journey together. It's not just me—we're all doing it, and we're all playing this game for a reason; we're here on this earth plane for a reason. What that reason is, we really don't know and it really doesn't matter. We can simply embrace the possibility and see if it works. If it does, hold on to it, and if it doesn't, discard it. Over and above that, really, what else do we need to know?

18

DISEMPOWERING OUR INNER CRITIC

Robert Augustus Masters

Self-acceptance is a great matter, asking much of us, and giving back even more. Exploring and cultivating intimacy with what's in the way of self-acceptance is an essential journey for us, if we are to truly come alive.

As a longtime health professional who has worked with many different types of people, I've come to see our collective challenge with self-acceptance as being strongly rooted in how we choose to view ourselves. We don't tend to cast a compassionate eye upon our weaknesses, our not-so-flattering places. Turning toward and gazing with compassion upon the qualities within us that don't make us feel good is a big step. To do this, to embody a deeper sense of self-acceptance, we have to come face to face with our inner critic or our internalized hub of toxic self-shaming.

Our inner critic is heartlessly negative self-appraisal. Its criticalness is far from healthy. Our inner critic is not a thing or an indwelling entity, but a doing, an activity, a process, ready to flare up and nail us with "shoulds" whenever we let it overpower us.

An initial step toward genuine self-acceptance is to be aware that our inner critic exists and is not about to leave town. We can no more eliminate it than we can eliminate our judging mind. We may think,

"Maybe I can get rid of it if I meditate more, do more therapy." No matter how hard we try, our inner critic does not go away.

The good news is that we can change how we relate to it. Once that happens, and we cease responding to the inner critic as if we are but a helpless child, it is still there but does not bother us in the same way, and may in fact become little more than occasional background noise.

The inner critic is like a mosquito. Mosquitos can be irritating when they get close, and may even overwhelm us when they get really close, buzzing, biting, and bothering us. However, when we deal skillfully with our inner critic, it becomes not much more than a mosquito on the far side of the room, almost out of hearing, not able to mess with us, not able to shame us.

When your inner critic kicks in, what's immediately helpful is to name it as such: "My inner critic is here" (or state the name you have given it). Then take a few deep breaths, softening your belly, distancing yourself from your inner critic's pronouncements, and observe its actual energy—as opposed to its contents and messages—and the resulting feelings that arise. Notice that the content of what your inner critic is saying—whatever its factual accuracy—is heartless, unkind, sometimes cruel, and always shaming.

We tend to turn into a child before our inner critic if we do not see it for what it is. We all have that child in us, no matter what our age, no matter how adult we may seem, and when we identify with the child within, our inner critic holds the power, talking to us as though we are but a child who keeps failing to meet certain standards. Note, however, that our inner critic does not hold the power inherently—*we* are giving it the power—the authority—to judge, shame, degrade us.

Once we sense the dynamic between our inner critic and our child side, which is usually just a repetitive drama of the bully and the bullied, healing can begin. We start to feel more intimate with—and more protective of—the child, whereas before, we mostly looked at the child in us through the eyes of our inner critic. So, if the child in us is shy, shut down in some way, hurting, or dysfunctional, we may have looked upon him or her with a sense of embarrassment—along the lines of "We shouldn't be that way. We're adults. We've worked on ourselves. How can we regress like that?" This only provides fuel for our inner critic. Then, it can announce, "Look at you. You're failing. You're weak. You're pathetic," and so on . . .

Unfortunately, for most of us, our inner critic masquerades as our conscience. The impression we get when it is speaking with such certainty and authority is that it is a valuable voice, perhaps even one that has our best interests at heart. One of its defining characteristics is that it has no heart. As we work to dis-identify with our inner critic and to cease being a child before it, we learn something very valuable: if we hear an internal voice that lacks compassion, lacks heart, we need not take its contents seriously.

As we acknowledge and observe our inner critic and step back from it, we need to move toward the child place in us—that locus of vulnerability, tenderness, innocence, and softness. We need to do what it takes to start loving that child, that part of us that is pre-rational, so young and tender, and so small. Once this happens, it brings out in us a sense of increased protectiveness, so that we are both embracing that little one and keeping him or her safe. At such times, the mosquito has flown to the other side of the room, perhaps so far that we can no longer hear it. It no longer has our ear.

We all have an inner critic. I grew up with a father who was very shaming and quick to find fault, and I internalized that, my sense of self-worth all but gone. I entered my early adult years with a heavy internalized sense of shame going full blast, crippling me in many ways. I learned to armor and mask this with aggression and overdone competitiveness, hugely overcompensating for the feeling of internal humiliation that plagued me. It took some very painful experiences in my twenties for me to begin cracking my hardness. When I did so, my aggression started fading—it became anger, coexisting with my hurt and shame.

Shame is the emotion at the core of the inner critic. Healthy shame triggers and is triggered by our conscience, but unhealthy shame—toxic shame—triggers and is triggered by our inner critic.

In my book *Emotional Intimacy*, I describe how we can become "intimate" with any emotion we might be experiencing. Being intimate with an emotional state means that we get really close to it, observing it in detail, but not so close that we lose focus or get overly absorbed by it.

If we are getting close to our shame, we are observing it in fine detail. We are not detached from it. We are not fleeing it or disowning it. We can sense our history with it and our future with it—what we are about to do or not do with it. There is a certain connection to it, but also a certain separation, too. Implicit in this, of course, is a lot of vulnerability. When we are intimate with a state, an emotion, or a person, we are in a position where we can be very hurt because we are so close, yet if we are not in close, we miss so much. That is true intimacy.

Sometimes when a difficult emotion arises—like fear or shame—we may decide to go right into it, feeling our way into its domain with curiosity and an explorer's spirit. We turn *toward* that emotion, taking our attentiveness into it, sensing its interiority as best we can, without getting lost in it.

Imagine seeing a child that has been hurt, your heart going out to that little one, your empathy on high. If, however, you get lost in his or her condition, you are not really going to be very helpful. If you can keep just a little bit of apartness, though, you can do first aid, call 911, comfort the child, and so on. This describes both the nature of intimacy and the way I work with people therapeutically—we are in so close to another's suffering that we cannot help but feel deep empathy for that one, yet we also have a subtle empathic wall in place so that we can still function skillfully.

We can learn to generate this quality of compassion toward ourselves. Take fear, for example. Fear is such a common emotion for most of us. When we get close to it, it is helpful to personify it as a distraught child, a frightened or terrified child that we can hold, embrace, and love. In this, we are bringing our fear into our heart, bit by bit. We are making room for it. To do this, we have to cultivate a willingness to turn toward what is difficult, painful, or challenging in our lives.

Try conceptualizing your fear as a closed fist. Visualize it thus. Now, imagine relaxing that hand, letting it soften and then open, the fingers effortlessly spreading. A subtle expansion occurs when we turn toward our fear and start to bring it into our heart. This expansion causes our fear to cease being so powerful, so gripping. When this happens, we may still be afraid, but we *do not mind* being afraid.

None of this is possible if we do not first learn to cultivate intimacy with our difficult states of being. A reason that real self-acceptance is such a challenge for us is because we have been conditioned to turn away from pain. We live in a culture devoted to the avoidance of pain—erotically, pharmaceutically, and so on. In all kinds of ways, our tendency—our default really—is to get away from pain when it arises.

It seems counterintuitive at first to turn toward our pain, but when we do, we have the opportunity to approach it, and slowly and consciously enter it. This means taking our conscious embodied attention into our pain and painful sensations and recognizing that it is a process always in flux. It's not that scary when we get inside it. The hardest part is turning toward it.

In my book *Spiritual Bypassing*, I talk about how people often use spirituality as a way to avoid their real experiences of pain. This is no big surprise because we tend to use other things in the same fashion. When we take up a spiritual practice, we may feel much better. "Wow, I can rise above my pain." We may even think the pain is not there. We may confuse transcendence with dissociation. There is a sense of being removed from or immune to our pain, but we are still avoiding it, and missing the profound learning that comes from truly facing our pain.

Real spirituality is about making room for everything within us to arise without any avoidance whatsoever. This is very difficult if we have not done some serious individual work, because sometimes what shows up can be profoundly frightening or disorienting. There is a litmus test for distinguishing between genuine transcendence and dissociation. In genuine transcendence, there is a sense of going beyond, but not excluding or dissociating from what has been gone beyond.

The key to this is intimacy, developing intimacy with all that we are. If we move past a certain stage of development, we do best to remain intimate with the previous stage. When it kicks in again—as it inevitably will—we recognize it and we are not enamored with being beyond it. In addition, if we are transcending something in a healthy way, we become more grounded, more compassionate, and more human. Our awakening is rich, vital, and embodied, requiring no disconnection from our emotions and humanness. Implicit in this is deep self-acceptance. Instead of abandoning what we don't like about ourselves, we infuse it with the kind of care that brings it into the circle of our being, thereby deepening our sense of wholeness.

One of the ways we can get a close look at our lack of self-acceptance is when we are in intimate relationship. Sometimes, something comes up that's quite challenging and perhaps even threatening to the relationship—maybe it's grief or rage or disappointment—and we become quite mental, instead of feeling and doing what it takes to reconnect with the other. We might give them advice, or something like that, which probably is not what they need. However, we can use such behavior not to put ourselves down, but to explore our own lack of self-acceptance. We may seem to be presenting something of value—perhaps offering some seemingly great advice—but what we are missing is connecting empathetically with the other, allowing ourselves to actually feel their grief, their discomfort, their shame. When this happens, when we give ourselves permission to emotionally resonate with that person, we can still keep a little bit of distance so we're not flooded by their state, and start reentering our intimacy with them.

The key here is to develop more compassion for our difficulty in accepting—not condoning, but accepting—where we are, noticing if our inner critic is giving us a hard time about this. We can then tell it, in whatever language we want, to "Stop!" or "Back the hell off" while we shift our awareness from thinking to feeling—from our head to our heart, belly, and legs—getting more and more grounded. It can help to let whomever we're with know that we are struggling and what we're doing about it.

This is especially helpful when we become vulnerable in our self-disclosure. Such transparent openness is contagious—it helps bring forward others in their vulnerability, so that they feel closer to us.

To do this effectively, we cannot allow ourselves to be detoured for long by shame, guilt, or some subtle embarrassment. Our work is, in part, to open our hearts to our closed-heartedness. In other words, to have compassion for the places in us that do not give a damn about what anyone else is experiencing. We all have a tendency to be me-centered and narcissistic, and we have the capacity to be we-centered and compassionate, without diminishing our individuality and autonomy.

Here is a practice you can use when you are holed up in your "head-quarters" and need to move more energy and presence into your heart:

- Shift your attention to your chest, breathing deeply into it. Soften your belly, keeping some awareness in both places at once.

- Once you've done this for a few minutes, bring some of that awareness into a younger place in yourself, a much younger version of you. Sense that you are there, perhaps frightened, perhaps shamed, but still aware.

- Bring that younger you, that little boy or girl, into your heart as best you can, and just breathe more presence into the space you are making for that child. Do not let your mind convince you to do otherwise, as in, "This is silly, I shouldn't be doing this." Just simply be with it. This causes a softening: the heart area, the shoulders, the face, your whole body softening, easing, and settling.

- Doing this, staying with this, generates a sense of reclaiming something that we might think we should have outgrown, but that is actually with us right through our entire lives—our innocence, our vulnerability, our pre-rational self. To turn away from the child in us simply impoverishes us.

There are some painful, dark, embarrassing things in each of us, things we can easily disown or reject or deny. When we move toward these things, approaching them with both care and curiosity, there is a sense of them leaving the shadows, shifting from being disowned or rejected *its* to reclaimed *me*. We can move toward becoming whole through such radical self-acceptance. Once this step has been taken a number of times, it becomes second nature to turn toward what is difficult or unpleasant, however small or hesitant our steps may be.

We can open our hearts to our own closed-heartedness by acknowledging to ourselves or to another person that we are closed-hearted, admitting this without self-shaming. You may tell yourself, "I feel disgust about this. I feel closed about that. My heart is shut down." Then, look at that very emotional state or quality through the eyes of something other than your inner critic.

Instead of perpetuating our self-shaming by rejecting and pulling away from the parts of ourselves that are seemingly messed up, turn toward them. When we do so, our heart begins going out to these parts, because we can sense the younger us in them, somewhere behind the scenes, wounded and unable to deal with the wound. This is not about excusing bad behavior, but about feeling into its roots with compassion. Real self-acceptance isn't about putting up with or tolerating bad behavior, but about bringing into our heart the one behind such behavior.

The process here is akin to going to a frightened child and being a loving space for them, holding them close—not telling them that everything's going to be okay, or that there's nothing wrong—and just being with them, presence-to-presence. In my trauma work with people, I find that there is always a part of them that is pre-rational, very vulnerable, and truly childlike—needing not to be fixed, but to be met with both care and protectiveness.

If we go back to our inner critic, there are many ways to respond to it. For example, I remember a client from some years ago who was suicidal because her inner critic wielded a megaphone seemingly without any off-switch—its voice was hugely forceful, relentless, and mean-spirited. It was not just a typical inner critic—this one was particularly vicious. Not surprisingly, this was exactly the way one of her parents had spoken to her when she was a child, and she had internalized it, reacting to it the same way she had reacted to her shaming parent—collapse. During one session, after we had done some deep work around this, she suddenly sat up, looked at me, and started to scream, "I am not you!" I knew she was talking to her inner critic. "I am not you! I am not you!" She kept doing it, and then stood up and began to almost dance. She got it! "I am not you; I am not my inner critic." She really took this in, and it changed her life in a very short time.

Our inner critic certainly can sound very convincing, but once we realize that it doesn't really care about us, we are on track to unseat it. It is a heartlessly negative appraisal of us, implanted in our childhood. The more that we understand its nature and recognize it when it takes center stage, the more easily we can say "No" to it and withdraw attention from its pronouncements. In doing this, we are no longer in its sway, no longer a child responding to a difficult parent. We are simply an adult, a healthy being, relating skillfully to an aspect of ourselves that is not so healthy.

Accomplishing this is about learning to directly relate to the not-so-healthy qualities in us, instead of letting them overrun or bully us, or trying to keep them out of sight. It comes back to intimacy, developing intimacy with all that we are, being able to keep a compassionate eye on all of our qualities, quirks, habitual ways of being. Think of intimacy as the poetry of relationship—with others and with parts of ourselves—it is the essence of connection, of genuine closeness.

When I was much younger, I had the ambition to get rid of the things in me that were not healthy—I meditated like a maniac and did a lot of therapy. Eventually, I realized that all my meditative experiences and all of the nonordinary states I could enter had not changed me at all. I still was the same insufferable person, padding my spiritual and psychological resumé. It was a sobering shock when I woke up one day and really got this. I realized that my work was to *relate* to these qualities and accept that they might stay with me throughout my life. There was no guarantee they were going to vanish simply because I did not want them or because I could do a meditative or therapeutic practice that made them seem like they were not there.

Nowadays, I do not mind my anger. I don't mind my fear. I don't mind my so-called bad qualities or neuroses. I just don't let them run the show. They are like kids that sit in the backseat while I drive. They play, and the inner critic is there, buzzing around like the mosquito it is and will always be, but nobody is bitten. Things can get chaotic in the backseat, but there's no real danger—unless I was to let one of the kids replace me at the wheel. Each of us is a collection, an assembly, and a community of selves. Our job is to be the presence that can hold them all in ways that help create a deeper sense of wholeness.

To reduce our inner critic to its proper size and buckle it into the backseat, we need to start with a clear sense of our history with our inner critic and its origins. Is it a reflection of one parent or the other, or a composite of both? Perhaps there was an older sibling who was harsh or cruel? A teacher? We need to get a sense of this and more, and to understand that our inner critic is an activity within us, ready to flare up when current conditions mimic the original conditions, which spawned our self-shaming tendencies.

For example, if we were overwhelmed by an angry parent who chronically slam-shamed us, part of our work would be to get in touch with the anger we had to repress in order to survive that parent's rages. If we have our anger on tap, we can say an effective "No" to our inner critic (which is also a no-longer-buried "No" to what our angry, shaming parent did to us). However, if we do not have our anger on tap, our "No" will be either nonexistent or anemic.

As we get a clearer sense of all this, we can start to talk *to* our inner critic. Perhaps this'll be in a Gestalt situation—our inner critic is in one chair, and we are across from them in the other chair—and going back and forth, a dialogue developing. Initially, a person will often speak in a tiny or weak voice to their inner critic, but with proper encouragement, they will eventually start to speak from their guts; will take firmer stands; will say "No" or "Stop" with increasingly adult firmness. As they do this, as they play their inner critic, it usually becomes weaker. They then start to realize, "My god, it's big and scary and seems so right, because I give it *my* power. I give it my attention. Now I'm going to starve it. I'm going to withdraw my attention and my energy from it. I'm not going to make the child in me face it—*I* will!"

We also need to recognize the aggression in the inner critic. Whether aggression is toward other people or ourselves, it is still aggression. And aggression and anger are not synonymous. We need to understand that anger is a natural, healthy emotion. It is a vulnerable, relational emotion, a moral emotion, but anger turns to aggression when we stop having compassion toward the subject of our anger and shift to simply being on the attack. Once we have done that, we have lost touch with the vulnerability and the relational component of anger; we are just out to get the other person; just like our inner critic attacking us.

Unfortunately, many of us on spiritual paths think that if we are angry we are not spiritual, but have simply regressed, slipping into an unwholesome state. Many Buddhist texts, for example, use the same word to translate ill will, hatred, aggression—and anger. Anger has gotten a lot of bad press, being automatically equated with aggression and violence. Therefore much of my work is to "re-vision" anger so that it becomes seen and experienced as a resource. The next concern is how to skillfully use it.

The key is vulnerability. If you are vulnerable in your anger with another person, they usually feel more at ease. I call this *heart-anger*, meaning fully expressed anger coexisting with some degree of compassion for the other person. To get to heart-anger we have to start with just regular anger, while remembering that we care about the other person (or ourselves) even when we are angry. We do not have to tone it down very much, or not have an angry face, but simply let the object of our anger know nonverbally that we are still with them, and that we are bothered by what they have done. We go after the behavior, not the person.

The inner critic, though, goes after the person, however much it may appear to be only addressing that person's behavior.

Many people think of their inner critic as a living entity, a kind of companion, but I see it as a personified verb or doing. We often conceive of our emotions as endogenous masses—*things* within that we can just simply get out of our system, things to merely vent or discharge. Not true! Emotion is not a thing, but a process. It is not just feeling—it is feeling, cognition, social factors, and conditioning all in dynamic interplay. Our inner critic is a kind of fluid conglomerate, too. There's emotion in it and cognition, plus a load of conditioning.

To return to the metaphor of the car, it is important to ask: "Who is driving it?" This touches the mystery of who and what we really are. If we ask "Who or what am I?" seriously and deeply enough, we come up with an answer that doesn't fit our usual notion of an "answer." It is often not a verbal answer—it is more a felt nonconceptual recognition, conveyed in a way that makes an unusual kind of sense. This is not abstract! It is somehow mysteriously individualized, far from some sort of depersonalized spirituality. There is a bedrock sense of it being the essential *you*, or the essential *me*.

Within that field of sentient presence, there are other elements that constitute *you* or *me*, like gender, occupation, childhood, and all of the different pieces of us. It is all in there, and it is a lovely thing to feel that nothing is excluded from this community. Entering more fully into the spirit of deep self-acceptance, we start to feel more intimate with our humanness and the human race, our drive to shift from fragmentation to wholeness.

Many spiritual teachers take up the question of *"What is our true nature?"* They may talk about it in various ways, perhaps as the ground of being, but will not necessarily point out the individualized sense, the essential "me-ness" in this ground of being. That essential me-ness or essential you-ness is not our ego. It's not the ego-centered dimensions of ourselves—it's our innate and ever-evolving uniqueness. No one has ever been born who is exactly like you or like me. We are each a unique flowering, here for just a short time, and hopefully blooming fully, with the capacity to bring together and accept all that we are: dual, nondual, and beyond.

The final stanza of a poem I once wrote goes like this:

> We are Light and we are Darkness
> And we are also the flesh
> Be it of mud or stars
> Born and torn between the two
> Yet already the One
> Inseparable
> From the broken Many

Consider the last two lines: *Inseparable / From the broken Many.* Often, we can be so caught up in spiritual and psychological ambition that we dissociate from the pain of others. The path I have chosen is the opposite. I let myself feel as much as possible, without getting lost in what I feel—not allowing my inner critic to get in the way, even as I accept its presence in me.

Self-acceptance is a great matter, asking much of us, and giving back even more. Exploring and cultivating intimacy with what's in the way of self-acceptance is an essential journey for us, if we are to truly come alive.

19

FAITH IN OUR
FUNDAMENTAL WORTHINESS

Sharon Salzberg

*The Buddha taught about things like generosity because they
gladden the mind and lead us to experience happiness, buoyancy,
and a sense of sufficiency, all of which strengthen our ability
for self-respect, self-kindness, and self-acceptance.*

I f, after I die, I am remembered for any contribution to Buddhism
in the West, it will probably be a conversation I had with His
Holiness the Dalai Lama in 1990 when I was at a Mind & Life
Institute conference in India. We were a part of a very small, private
gathering, where I was lucky to have the opportunity to ask him a
question. My approach was direct: I simply walked up to him and
asked, "Your Holiness, what do you think about self-hatred?"

With a perplexed expression, he replied, "What's that?"

This answer was, and still is, fantastic. His lack of familiarity with
the notion of "self-hatred" could not have been any more genuine.

Unsurprisingly, His Holiness followed up with a series of puzzled
questions: "Is that some kind of nervous disorder? Are people like that
very violent?" He and I engaged in a sustained back and forth, until he
interrupted with a revelatory thought: "But we have Buddha Nature. And
you have Buddha Nature—how could you think of yourself that way?"
He just didn't get that common struggle many of us know as self-loathing.

My favorite part of that whole exchange actually happened *after* it was over. We were taking a tea break and some of the Dalai Lama's Western translators gathered around him. They approached him, saying things like, "Your Holiness, when we read in the teachings something like, 'Give up all self-cherishing,' we think it means something like 'Stop caring about yourself.'" It was a fascinating cultural conversation because in Buddhist teachings (particularly in translations of Tibetan texts) the imperative to "Give up self-cherishing" refers more to the sacrifice of self-preoccupation, obsession with oneself. Instead, we're encouraged to develop an interest in others, and in the situation of others, to develop compassion for others.

Westerners misconstrue the wisdom to "Give up self-cherishing" to mean something more like, "Don't care about yourself at all." We miss the part where we consider how the *motivation* behind any action is such a crucial element of that action. For instance, people might receive a teaching like "Stop self-cherishing" and immediately think they need to give up all things that add value to their lives, in favor of some sense of self-deprecation. They may think, "I'm going to give up everything. I'm going to give away everything I have." Yet, this impulse toward self-denial does not emerge from a sense of oneness with everyone. Rather, it comes from self-deprecation: "I don't deserve to have anything; I shouldn't have anything; I shouldn't own anything; I don't deserve to be happy; and I'm just going to give everything away."

Classically, this kind of "giving away" would not even be considered generosity, as it's coming from such a pained and unsettled place. By contrast, it's almost assumed in the Buddhist teachings that we're coming from a place of some self-respect and even celebration of that capacity to have love and compassion, understanding, and connection. It's for this reason that Westerners often have to take a step back and build a different foundation to re-contextualize many of these ideas and pieces of wisdom.

There are indeed cultural roots for these deeply rooted feelings of self-blame and self-condemnation that so many of us experience. And I imagine that even if one doesn't come from a particular religious background, this pattern still comes from our tendency to reify "the self" as something fixed, and feel a coexisting sense of separation, or alienation from the truth of change.

This resistance to embracing change—both in terms of the self, and in our experiences—ties into the idea of forgiveness (and self-forgiveness), the ever-present option to begin again, surprisingly, without guilt. In Buddhist systems of morality, if you make a mistake, violate a precept or the harmony of a community, or have caused suffering for yourself or someone else, the thing to do is simply to recognize that mistake, not decide, "I'm a terrible person, and I always will be."

The Buddhist moral compass would instead point you toward self-awareness: to recognize the error, to feel the pain of it, and to use that to move forward toward greater understanding and different behavior. In the aftermath of such a mistake or error, a Buddhist would say, "Well, you need to take the precept again." That's a very different tone from the way we, in our culture, tend to spiral down into a terrible tunnel of guilt and self-blame, causing ourselves to think things like, "I'm a horrible person, and always will be. I don't have the capacity to change because I am just like this. There is no change . . . "

The potential for the introduction of meditation and alternative self-examination practices to reshape this Western understanding is still in its pioneering stage, I think. The context and the environment within which Westerners engage these practices is in flux. For example, in Asia, you typically work quite closely with a teacher—with a personal teacher—and are not left to your own devices to try to figure things out. You have a teacher who may (not always so politely) say, "For God's sake, relax! Take a walk! Stop meditating!" or whatever the necessary lesson might be at a particular time. They might send you off to do some kind of service, perhaps based on the particular challenges you are undergoing—not as a punishment, but as an opportunity to cultivate the practice of generosity. "Go into the marketplace, the world, and see what happens in your mind and heart as you begin to share or model the teachings." This is part of the meditation practice; it's not just about sitting there. In this way, meditation is not just a method to reduce stress and grow focused (though it works for those things, too).

I had one teacher, a Burmese monk named Sayadaw U Pandita, who was extremely demanding and fierce, but also astoundingly supportive. His intensity as a teacher always made me think, "Wow . . . he thinks I can do it. He thinks I can really accomplish something in this retreat. He thinks I can really go further than I've gone before." Even though his methodology was disciplined and rigorous, it didn't feel like harshness to me. It simply felt like what it was: an invitation to try harder, because he believed I could. And I could. I trusted him. I believe his motivation was necessary for me. It wasn't about his egotistical needs at all—and so the dynamic absolutely worked. I knew I could really put in more effort than I was used to at that stage of my practice and see where it took me, so I did.

In this case, the dedication was all about the inspiration. Of course, inspiration can manifest in many ways—but it comes potently from somebody believing in you. Whether it is a mentor, or even a peer, having somebody who looks at us with faith and conviction allows us to absorb that energy. That's what helps push us along in our practice. Whether it is a person who is reflecting something back on us, or an awakening inside of us that we can take a step, that we can try, that we can not be stuck, that we can be different—that life can be different—that's faith. Without faith, we'd be completely inert. Without faith, we wouldn't do anything, even if we *could*.

Likewise, I think devotion is essential, because we never really arrive at any place alone. We are all part of this fabric of life. One of my favorite little activities to do whenever I'm with a small group is to ask everyone to bring to mind anyone who they think might be involved with the fact that they're sitting there in the room at that moment. It might be the person who gave you a book or a CD, or who read you a poem, or told you a story about their meditation practice. By just seeing who comes to mind, we realize that every moment of our lives is a confluence of connection—that we're all in that room, in that moment, because of conversations and relationships and encounters and challenges and all sorts of other things.

Every moment is rich. I think this also relates to that habit of self-hatred, self-judgment, or self-criticism. Whatever these habits look like to each of us, they tend to happen because we neglect to recognize each moment as rich, an opportunity to reflect on the intense connection that pervades life. Instead, we view ourselves as somehow cut off or isolated from the rest of the world. A sneaky—and often effective—way to work with this habit of self-hatred is to recognize the more insidious worldview(s) that might be feeding it, and to challenge it.

In my book *Faith*, I tell a story about going to do a retreat a few years ago with friends in Martha's Vineyard, where I had an unexpected lesson on the topic of "self-hatred." In my bedroom, there was a cartoon from the *Peanuts* comic strip. In the first panel, Lucy approaches Charlie Brown, and tells him, "You know, Charlie Brown, the problem with you is that you're *you*." In the second frame, poor Charlie Brown looks at her and responds, "Well, what in the world can I do about that?" In the third (and final) frame Lucy sarcastically concludes, "I don't pretend to be able to give advice; I merely point out the problem." Whenever I looked at the cartoon, my eye would fall right on that line, "The problem with you is that you're *you*."

I would say that from the time I was a child; that "Lucy voice" was the dominant voice in my life. The Lucy voice is arguably the voice of self-hatred. It's the voice that silences your aspirational side and tells you, "You can't really do anything because you don't know how." I had such a confused childhood with so many people dying or leaving and so much transition, that I think the predominant reality of my life was that I felt fragmented. I was disconnected and confused, and so my Lucy voice got very strong.

Then, when I was eighteen, I went to India and began the process of cultivating my meditation practice. It was a combination of my relationship with my teachers and the actual practice that helped me diminish my feeling of fragmentation. It also served to give me a way to deal with that Lucy voice so that it became something I could recognize, with a keen observational eye, as quite horrifying. I began to recognize how damaging that kind of self-criticism was for me. I didn't rebel against the Lucy voice, but learned ways of working with, rather than against, it. Through Buddhist practice, I found that the more I could actually have some kindness and compassion toward Lucy, the less important it became that she might show up. It was about adopting a more complete, flexible, and balanced sense of who I am and what I care about. With this new mindset, my Lucy voice was no longer my enemy, but a guest I could invite in. It was this shift in view that changed the dynamic with my Lucy voice.

Some people might refer to Lucy as their "inner critic"—I do. The hardest thing for me is when I feel I have made a mistake. Especially if I've hurt somebody or haven't done something as well as I could have, my mind starts that spiral. I can measure the degree of my suffering by the length of time it takes me to have a more kindly attitude toward my guilt or let go of it. It doesn't serve us to be afraid of what comes up in our mind even if what's coming up is that tremendously critical Lucy voice. Seeing it as fixed and unchanging, as an inarguable enemy, doesn't work.

Not only do we *not* recognize kindness and acceptance (this includes self-kindness and self-acceptance) as powerful skills, but we tend to think of them as secondary virtues. Many of us perpetuate the cultural assumption that if we can't embody a primary virtue like courage, boldness, or brilliance, then we can simply fall back on being kind—because anyone can do it.

This is a false assumption. Kindness is so much more powerful than that. It really is like a force—*and* it's a skill. It's not as if some people have it and other people don't. Although some people have had lives with more reassurance and positive feedback than others, every single one of us has the ability to cultivate kindness. Certainly, kindness may come more readily to some and feel more difficult for others to develop. But, ultimately, it is a skill that all of us can grow more deeply into—because cultivating kindness is a matter of training our attention.

There are times when we think getting down on ourselves is a good thing. We might think, "That's how we learn. That's how we make change." We don't always see the cost and how guilt is debilitating us, but the more we can pay attention, the more we recognize the cost of our lack of self-acceptance. Then, we can develop the skills to reach for change from a different, deeper place—to give Lucy a cup of tea and send her on her way.

The core competencies we need to start developing this skill of self-kindness are:

- *Mindfulness:* Know what you're feeling.
- *Wisdom:* Step back from what you're feeling so you have some perspective.
- *Intention:* Be open to experimenting and having little adventures of consciousness.

We can do this by making kind and generous promises to ourselves, the same way we might to those we care about. We can choose, as a practice, to say to ourselves, "Okay, I'm going to thank three people today." Or, "I'm going to thank myself." Or, "I'm going to notice when I've made a mistake and I'm going to try to come back more gently and start over." These little things punctuate our world of habit, but they take intention. They're not going to come just because we think it's a good idea. Intention implies the presence of choice, agency, will. That's what the mind can do: make choices, harness agency and will.

Happiness is, therefore, a choice. It is not some passive state we fall into, but a state we can choose to cultivate. There's a nice phrase in Buddhist teaching that's rarely used in the West: *gladdening the mind.* The Buddha taught about things like generosity because they gladden the mind and lead us to experience happiness, buoyancy, and a sense of sufficiency—all of which strengthen our ability for self-respect, self-kindness, and self-acceptance. When we practice morality, we're less likely to get freaked out or paranoid, wondering, "What if they find out the terrible thing I did?", which also gladdens the mind. To gladden the mind is to recognize that the mind doesn't simply control us. We can recognize what it is doing and what it is not doing, and so change the dynamic between self-criticism and self-acceptance through practice—just like we can change any other habit.

As Buddhists, we don't look at suffering in any of its manifestations—including self-hatred—with the idea that we want to just suffer. That's not the point! The point is to discover what joins us to a greater whole through compassion, even as we face suffering. It's to gladden the mind. Ours is a whole path that leads us to be able to disentangle the great question of "Who am I?" and to look directly at pleasure, suffering, and all matter of things.

REFERENCES

Blackstone, Judith. *Belonging Here: A Guide for the Spiritually Sensitive Person*. Boulder, CO: Sounds True, 2012.

Chödrön, Pema. *Start Where You Are: A Guide to Compassionate Living*. Boston: Shambhala Classics, 2001.

Douglas-Klotz, Neil. *Prayers of the Cosmos: Meditations on the Aramaic Words of Jesus*. New York: Harper One, 2009.

Hawkins, David R. *Letting Go: The Pathway of Surrender*. Carlsbad, CA: Hay House, 2014.

Hayes, Stephen C., Kirk D. Strosahl, and Kelly G. Wilson. *Acceptance and Commitment Therapy, Second Edition: The Process and Practice of Mindful Change*. New York: The Guilford Press, 2011.

Krishnamurti, Jiddu. *The First and Last Freedom*. New Delhi: Rajpal & Sons, 2013.

Luoma, J. B., B. S. Kohlenberg, S. C. Hayes, and L. Fletcher. "Slow and Steady Wins the Race: A Randomized Clinical Trial of Acceptance and Commitment Therapy Targeting Shame in Substance Use Disorders." *Journal of Consulting and Clinical Psychology* 80 (2012): 43–53.

Masters, Robert Augustus. *Emotional Intimacy: A Comprehensive Guide for Connecting with the Power of Your Emotions*. Boulder, CO: Sounds True, 2013.

Masters, Robert Augustus. *Spiritual Bypassing: When Spirituality Disconnects Us from What Really Matters.* Berkeley, CA: North Atlantic Books, 2010.

Neff, Kristin. *Self-Compassion: Stop Beating Yourself Up and Leave Insecurity Behind.* New York: Morrow, 2010.

Repacholi, Betty M., and Alison Gopnik. "Early Reasoning about Desires: Evidence from 14- and 18-Month-Olds." *Developmental Psychology* 33 (1997): 12–21.

Rilke, Rainer Maria. *Rilke's Book of Hours: Love Poems to God.* Translated by Anita Barrows and Joanna Macy. New York: Penguin, 2005.

Salzberg, Sharon. *Faith: Trusting Your Own Experience.* New York: Riverhead, 2003.

Shapira, L. B., and M. Mongrain. "The Benefits of Self-Compassion and Optimism Exercises for Individuals Vulnerable to Depression." *The Journal of Positive Psychology* 5 (2010): 377–89.

Tipping, Colin C., and JoAnn Tipping. *Radical Manifestation: The Fine Art of Creating the Life You Want.* Marietta, GA: Global 13 Publishing, 2008.

ABOUT THE CONTRIBUTORS

Judith Blackstone, PhD, is a spiritual teacher and psychotherapist. She developed the Realization Process, a method of embodied nondual awakening and psychological healing, and teaches it worldwide. She is a founding director of Nonduality Institute. She is the author of *Belonging Here, The Enlightenment Process, The Intimate Life,* and *The Empathic Ground.* An audio series of *The Realization Process* is available from Sounds True. Find out more about Judith's teachings at RealizationCenter.com.

Tara Brach, PhD, has been practicing and teaching meditation since 1975, as well as leading Buddhist meditation retreats and workshops in North America and Europe. She is a clinical psychologist, the founder of the Insight Meditation Community of Washington (IMCW), and the author of *Radical Acceptance* and *True Refuge: Finding Peace and Freedom in Your Own Awakened Heart.* To learn more about her work, please visit TaraBrach.com.

Raphael Cushnir is a leading voice in the world of emotional connection and present moment awareness. He has shared his unique approach to personal and professional development with millions of readers in *O, The Oprah Magazine; Beliefnet; Spirituality and Health; Psychology Today;* and *The Huffington Post.* He is the author of six books, lectures worldwide, and is a faculty member of the Esalen Institute, the Kripalu Center for Yoga & Health, and the Omega Institute for Holistic Studies. In addition, he coaches individuals and teams at Fortune 100 companies, governments, religious organizations, and leading nonprofits. Raphael's website is Cushnir.com.

Jay Earley, PhD, is a transformational psychologist, group leader, psychotherapist, teacher, and theorist. He is a specialist in IFS Therapy and has taught hundreds of people how to use this system for their personal growth. Jay is the author of *Self-Therapy, Freedom from Your Inner Critic, The Pattern System*, and *Self-Therapy* audio training. He is the creator of Self-Therapy Journey, an online tool for personal growth and psychological healing. For more information on the IFS programs, please see Personal-Growth-Programs.com.

Jeff Foster studied astrophysics at Cambridge University. Following a period of depression and physical illness, he embarked on an intensive spiritual quest that ended with the discovery that life itself—the present moment—was what he had always been seeking. He now travels the world, speaking about the journey of healing and spiritual awakening, inviting exhausted seekers to come to rest in presence. With Sounds True, Jeff has published a book and an audio program, both titled *The Deepest Acceptance: Radical Awakening in Ordinary Life*. His website is LifeWithoutACentre.com.

Rick Hanson, PhD, is a psychologist, a senior fellow of the Greater Good Science Center at University of California–Berkeley, and a *New York Times* bestselling author. His books include *Hardwiring Happiness* and *Just One Thing* (both published in fourteen languages), *Buddha's Brain* (published in twenty-five languages), and *Mother Nurture*. He edits the *Wise Brain Bulletin* and has created several audio programs. As a founder of the Wellspring Institute for Neuroscience and Contemplative Wisdom, he's been an invited speaker at Oxford, Stanford, and Harvard Universities, and he's taught in meditation centers worldwide. Rick's work has been featured on the BBC, CBS, and NPR, and he offers the *Just One Thing* newsletter and the online Foundations of Well-Being program in positive neuroplasticity. Find out more at RickHanson.net.

Steven C. Hayes received his PhD in clinical psychology from West Virginia University in 1977 and is currently a Nevada Foundation professor in the Department of Psychology at the University of Nevada, Reno. The author of forty-one books and nearly 580 scientific articles, his interests cover basic research, applied research, methodology, and philosophy of science. His career has focused on an analysis of the nature of human language and cognition, and the application of this to the understanding and alleviation of human suffering. Please visit StevenCHayes.com.

Harville Hendrix, PhD, and **Helen LaKelly Hunt, PhD,** are partners in life and work. They believe that how we interact with each other—within family, workplace, communities—is the key to emotional, physical, and economic well-being. They envision the possibility of shifting from the Age of the Individual to the Age of Relationship. To make relational information and skills available to everyone, the couple co-initiated Imago Relationships International, which offers workshops, training programs, lectures, seminars, and books.

In addition, the couple's professional partnership has produced ten books, including three *New York Times* bestsellers: *Getting the Love You Want, Keeping the Love You Find,* and *Giving the Love that Heals.* Their most recent book is *Making Marriage Simple.*

Harville is a couple's therapist with more than forty years of experience as an educator, clinical trainer, and lecturer. His work was featured eighteen times on *Oprah.* Helen is the author of *Faith and Feminism* and creator of Women Moving Millions, an organization that raises funds for the advancement of women and girls. For her work with philanthropic entrepreneurism and leadership in the global women's movement, she was inducted into the Women's Hall of Fame. Helen and Harville have been married for more than thirty years, have six children, and reside in Dallas, Texas. Their website is HarvilleAndHelen.com.

Robert Augustus Masters, PhD, is an integral psychotherapist, relationship expert, and spiritual teacher whose work blends the psychological and physical with the spiritual—emphasizing embodiment, emotional literacy, and the development of relational maturity. He is the author of thirteen books, including *Transformation through Intimacy, Spiritual Bypassing,* and his most recent book from Sounds True, *To Be a Man: A Guide to True Masculine Power.* You can find Robert's essays and poetry at RobertMasters.com.

Kelly McGonigal, PhD, is a health psychologist and award-winning lecturer at Stanford University. A leading expert on the mind-body relationship, her work integrates the latest findings of psychology, neuroscience, and medicine with contemplative practices of mindfulness and compassion from the traditions of Buddhism and yoga. She is the author of *The Willpower Instinct* and *Yoga for Pain Relief.* Learn about her work with stress at KellyMcGonigal.com.

Karla McLaren, MEd, is an award-winning author, social science researcher, and pioneering educator whose empathic approach to emotions revalues even the most "negative" emotions and opens startling new pathways into the depths of the soul. Karla is the author of the books and audio learning programs *The Art of Empathy: A Complete Guide to Life's Most Essential Skill,* and *The Language of Emotions: What Your Feelings Are Trying to Tell You,* and the online video course *Emotional Flow: Becoming Fluent in the Language of Emotions.* She is also the developer of Dynamic Emotional Integration®, a nonclinical approach to emotional health and empathic awareness. For more information, visit KarlaMcLaren.com.

Dr. Kristin Neff is an Associate Professor of Human Development and Culture at the University of Texas at Austin. In addition to her pioneering research into self-compassion, she has developed an eight-week program to teach self-compassion skills. The program, co-created with her colleague Chris Germer at Harvard University, is called *Mindful Self-Compassion.* Her book titled *Self-Compassion* was published by William Morrow in April 2011. She is also the creator of the Sounds True audio learning course *Self-Compassion Step by Step.* Kristin and her family were also the subjects of the 2009 documentary and book *The Horse Boy,* which chronicled her family's journey to Mongolia to find healing for their son. You'll find self-compassion meditations and exercises at Self-Compassion.org.

Mark Nepo is the #1 *New York Times* bestselling author of *The Book of Awakening.* Beloved as a poet, teacher, and storyteller, Mark has been called "one of the finest spiritual guides of our time." He has published sixteen books and recorded eleven audio projects, and his work has been translated into more than twenty languages. Mark has appeared several times with Oprah Winfrey on her *Super Soul Sunday* program on OWN TV, and has also been interviewed by Robin Roberts on *Good Morning America*. Sounds True is the publisher of his book *Inside the Miracle: Enduring Suffering, Approaching Wholeness*, and has released three of his audio programs: *Staying Awake: The Ordinary Art, Holding Nothing Back: Essentials for an Authentic Life*, and *Reduced to Joy: The Journey from Our Head to Our Heart*. You can read some of his poetry at MarkNepo.com.

Erin Olivo, PhD, MPH, is a licensed clinical psychologist with more than twenty years of experience treating patients. In addition, she is an assistant clinical professor of medical psychology at Columbia University's College of Physicians and Surgeons. She was formerly the Director of the Columbia Integrative Medicine Program, which she headed in collaboration with Dr. Mehmet Oz. Erin is the author of *Wise Mind Living: Master Your Emotions, Transform Your Life*. Visit her website at ErinOlivo.com.

Geneen Roth's pioneering books were among the first to link compulsive eating and perpetual dieting with deeply personal and spiritual issues that go far beyond food, weight, and body image. She believes that we eat the way we live, and that our relationship to food, money, and love is an exact reflection of our deepest-held beliefs about ourselves and the amount of joy, abundance, pain, and scarcity we believe we have—or are allowed to have—in our lives. She is the author of nine books, including the #1 *New York Times* bestsellers *Women Food and God, Lost and Found,* and *When Food Is Love*. Geneen has appeared on many national television shows including: *Oprah, 20/20, The NBC Nightly News, The View, The Today Show,* and *Good Morning America*. Articles about Geneen and her work have appeared in numerous publications including: *O: The Oprah Magazine, Cosmopolitan, Time, Elle, The New York Times,* and *The Chicago Tribune*. Her website is GeneenRoth.com.

Sharon Salzberg, a student of Buddhism since 1971, has been leading meditation retreats worldwide since 1974. Influenced by her more than twenty-five years of study with Burmese, Indian, and Tibetan teachers, she teaches intensive awareness practice (Vipassana, or insight meditation) and the profound cultivation of lovingkindness and compassion (the Brahma Viharas). She is a cofounder of the Insight Meditation Society and The Barre Center for Buddhist Studies, both in Massachusetts. Salzberg is the author of several books including *The Kindness Handbook, Faith: Trusting Your Own Deepest Experience, Lovingkindness: The Revolutionary Art of Happiness, A Heart as Wide as the World, Real Happiness at Work,* and the *New York Times* bestseller *Real Happiness.* She has also authored several Sounds True audio and interactive learning kit works including *Insight Meditation* (with Joseph Goldstein), *Unplug,* and *Lovingkindness Meditation.* Learn more at SharonSalzberg.com.

Friedemann Schaub, MD, PhD, is a physician specializing in cardiology and a molecular biologist who has helped thousands of people to overcome fear and anxiety with his breakthrough and empowerment program, which combines his medical expertise with NLP, Time Line Therapy™, clinical hypnotherapy, meditation, and more. He is the author of the book *The Fear and Anxiety Solution,* an in-depth resource to complement his audio program of the same title. Learn more at his website, TheFearAndAnxietySolution.com.

Bruce Tift, MA, LMFT, has been in private practice since 1979, taught at Naropa University for twenty-five years, and has given presentations in the United States, Mexico, and Japan. A practitioner of Vajrayana Buddhism for more than forty years, he had the good fortune to be a student of Chögyam Trungpa Rinpoche and to meet a number of realized teachers. Sounds True has published his book *Already Free: Buddhism Meets Psychotherapy on the Path of Liberation,* and the same-titled companion audio program.

Colin Tipping was born in England and taught at London University before immigrating to the United States in 1984. With his wife, JoAnn, he cofounded the Georgia Cancer Help Program and Together-We-Heal, Inc., and founded The Institute for Radical Forgiveness Therapy and Coaching. Colin is the author of the international bestseller *Radical Forgiveness: Making Room for the Miracle* and other books and online programs based on the practice of Radical Forgiveness. With Sounds True, he has released six programs related to his radical forgiveness work. Please visit RadicalForgiveness.com.

ABOUT SOUNDS TRUE

Sounds True is a multimedia publisher whose mission is to inspire and support personal transformation and spiritual awakening. Founded in 1985 and located in Boulder, Colorado, we work with many of the leading spiritual teachers, thinkers, healers, and visionary artists of our time. We strive with every title to preserve the essential "living wisdom" of the author or artist. It is our goal to create products that not only provide information to a reader or listener, but that also embody the quality of a wisdom transmission.

For those seeking genuine transformation, Sounds True is your trusted partner. At SoundsTrue.com you will find a wealth of free resources to support your journey, including exclusive weekly audio interviews, free downloads, interactive learning tools, and other special savings on all our titles.

To learn more, please visit SoundsTrue.com/freegifts or call us toll-free at 800.333.9185.

SOUNDS TRUE
many voices, one journey